Charles Anderson's quest of the A_____ ble *evidence of the very traits that serv_* to *France for thirty-three years. Both e_* fi- *culties, obstacles, and discourageme._ _____ .quired vanquishing cravings for comfort and self-indulgence. Endurance was a major ingredient in one as in the other. Charles' focus in each mission was service for his Savior.* Beyond My Limits *is a clarion call to step beyond the ordinary in life and in service.*

—Dr. Gary L. Anderson
President, Baptist Mid-Missions, Cleveland, Ohio

Ironically, even people who hike a wilderness to get away from other people feel a special bond for people they meet in the wilderness. Carry a backpack that far or that high without whining and you are accepted! Problem is, many who follow arduous trails expertly have lost their way in the terrain of life. That is why Charles Anderson, hiking the Appalachian Trail, carried more than a map and a compass. He carried God's Word. I highly recommend Charles' amazing diary, Beyond My Limits. *Read it and discover how readily any venture in life can become an avenue of service for God.*

—Don Richardson
Author of *Peace Child, Lords of the Earth,
Eternity in Their Hearts,* and other works

Having known Charles for fifty years, I can assure you that the lessons he has gleaned and shares in Beyond My Limits *will be gems from the heart of a seasoned missionary.*

—George Theis
Former Executive Director of Word of Life International

Missionaries never take time for themselves. So, when Charles Anderson squeezed a Bible into his backpack and started hiking toward Maine's Mt. Katahdin two thousand miles away, his family and friends cheered. No one doubted that he would make it, and my friend has once again proven that he can fulfill an assignment. Charles' example will lead to more than the top of a mountain. The message he makes known will lead to eternal life.

—Norman Rohrer
Founder, the Christian Writers Guild

Charles Anderson

Beyond
My Limits

ADVENTURES WITH GOD
ON THE APPALACHIAN TRAIL

WinePressPublishing
Great Books, Defined.

WinePress Publishing (PO Box 428, Enumclaw, WA 98022) functions only as book publisher. As such, the ultimate design, content, editorial accuracy, and views expressed or implied in this work are those of the author.

Unless otherwise noted, all Scriptures are taken from the *New King James Version*, © 1979, 1980, 1982 by Thomas Nelson, Inc., Publishers. Used by permission.

Scripture references marked KJV are taken from the *King James Version* of the Bible.

ISBN 13: 978-1-60615-020-7
ISBN 10: 1-60615-020-0
Library of Congress Catalog Card Number: 2009934534

To Babs:
Girl of my dreams, wise and unfailing helpmate, courageous companion in the adventures God planned for us long before that first twinkle in our eyes.

To Chad, David, and Mark:
You guys have brought more excitement and satisfaction to your father than he ever dreamed. May God lead you in paths of righteousness as you climb mountains and walk through valleys following His perfect plan for your lives. Onward!

Contents

Foreword

It is fitting that the Christian journey through life is described as a walk. As Charles Anderson takes us along on his walk of the entire Appalachian Trail, he makes it clear that it is no walk in the park, where all is made convenient and comfortable. No, the walk we take in these pages, like the one we all take through life, takes us through craters and swamps, up rugged mountains, to narrow defiles, and occasionally into pleasant meadows.

This book is far more than a travelogue or a guide for other trail walkers. It is not an adventure story that never penetrates beyond the risks of the route. It becomes the portrait of a man and his pilgrimage of self-discovery as he worships in the wonders of what the Creator has made. But even in the midst of such indescribable beauty . . . and the fatigue and the mosquitoes and the blisters and the little triumphs that make it worth the effort, Charles encounters people. Each person is a story in progress. The natural camaraderie of the trail creates an intimacy that encourages people to open up, to face the reality of who they are—and are not—before God and each other.

Every hiker who resolves to tackle the whole Appalachian Trail has his or her own reasons for doing so. A few conquer it in a single season, while most scatter the adventure through several seasons or their whole lifetime. It is a major accomplishment that no one will applaud except the few who know the agonies and expectations of a family member or close friend. But this is not a conquest of the final peak. It is a process of struggles, doubts, exhilarations, and encounters that enrich a person because of all that is overcome along the way.

Come walk with Charles. Feel the friction of his backpack, the rocks under his hiking boots, the frustrations of tough circumstances, and the solitude of worship in the woods. Enjoy the friendship of fellow pilgrims and the openness to share spiritual insights, getting beyond God as Creator to Jesus Christ as Savior. Smell the smoky campfires, the perfume of wildflowers, and the joy of serving the Lord by helping others along the way and being encouraged by them. This is not the setting where his many years in the gospel ministry in France and elsewhere are impressive. What counts is the joy of meeting people, the joy of walking with God, and the joy of knowing that Charles moves toward a final destination far more glorious than Mount Katahdin. Let's go walking!

—Dr. Bill Smallman
First Vice-President, Baptist Mid-Missions
Cleveland, Ohio

The Appalachian Trail

Preface

Beads of sweat roll down my face and drip off my nose and chin as I climb out of Horse Gap, ten miles north of Springer Mountain, Georgia, the starting point of the Appalachian Trail. "Horse Gap," even the name seems to mock me, implying I'm no more than a beast of burden. Overwhelming fatigue and feelings of defeat dog my steps. Aching muscles whimper, "You can't do this!"

The message of my muscles that second day on the trail would echo a thousand times before I finished my 2,000-mile odyssey. The story of my hike of the Appalachian Trail is a tale of the grace of God that enabled me to venture far beyond my limits, both physically and spiritually. I was on a mission: a mission of faith with the goal of sharing the message of Christ with as many hikers as I could. I would learn a new language, adapt to a new culture, take more risks and face more dangers than I ever took or faced before, and beyond that, would grapple with spiritual forces determined to derail my mission. But in the end, the Appalachian Trail would become a path of discovery, witness, and adventure more exciting and rewarding than I ever imagined.

I was not exactly a stranger to the outdoors. I had made visits to the wilderness, but I had never lived in it. That changed dramatically as I section-hiked the Trail over a period of nine years, from my shortest hike of 30 miles, to my longest of 560 miles. The Appalachian Trail eventually became my great friend, my home in the wilderness, and one of the passions of my life.

To millions of Americans, the Appalachian Trail is the quintessence of adventure and challenge. Mention the Appalachian Trail (AT) to a group of friends, and chances are that eyes will light up and ears will perk up. The mystic and the magic surrounding the AT are perhaps hard to explain, but they are undeniably there.

The AT is approximately 2,160 miles long and winds northward from Georgia to Maine, passing through fourteen states: Georgia, North Carolina, Tennessee, Virginia, West Virginia, Maryland, Pennsylvania, New Jersey, New York, Massachusetts, Connecticut, Vermont, New Hampshire, and Maine. The Trail takes the hiker over mountains (650 to be exact) across streams, through enchanting forests, and by way of flowered meadows. The landscape is so varied and beautiful that I was never bored. A common misconception needs to be laid to rest: the AT is rarely a gentle path through the woods. The reality is that the AT often straddles the most rugged terrain in eastern United States.

Basic to any human endeavor or experience are people. It was my privilege to walk and talk with hundreds of fascinating people, from Georgia to Maine. I met some of America's most outstanding young people. Each encounter changed or challenged me in some way. I still pray for many of the hikers I met.

On my hike, I rediscovered America. Having lived in France as a missionary for thirty-three years, I had lost touch with my own country. Walking through its vastness, its beauty, and its small towns, I gained a profound appreciation for the greatness of America and a new understanding of how much God has blessed this nation, perhaps more than any other in the world.

The story of my Appalachian Trail hike was recorded day by day in small, spiral-bound notebooks that, when stacked on my desk, make a hefty pile. It is my privilege to share this amazing experience with you. I invite you to slip into comfortable hiking boots and walk with me on an AT adventure. May your discoveries be like mine, exciting and life-changing.

Chapter 1

Birth of a Passion

But the path of the just is like the shining sun.
—Proverbs 4:18

E arly September, 1952: It was the beginning of the Eisenhower era, and the world was a peaceful place. It was also my senior year of high school in the steel mill town of Warren, Ohio.

I walked into the crowded homeroom of my senior class and was greeted by a loud chorus of voices. To the bookworms and class achievers, the noise signaled the excitement of a new school year; but to the rest of us, it meant only the end of swimming, tennis, and hanging out with friends—and a return to the dreary routine of school.

"Let's get this over with," I thought and groaned, already anticipating my graduation the following year.

After making my way through the milling students, I reached the table where the As sat—Adams, Adgate, Andrews, Anderson—and dumped my few books on the heavy oak table and slumped into a chair. Looking around at nothing in particular, I had no inkling that in the next few minutes something would happen so important that it would capture my imagination and profoundly affect my life four decades later. Several tables away, I noticed a half-dozen students standing around a classmate named Ray, listening with rapt attention.

Well-dressed Ray was an excellent student and a class leader. Curious about what had captured the students' interest, I left my seat and elbowed my way in to the small group. Straining above the classroom noise to hear what Ray was saying so enthusiastically, I caught the words "hiking," "Pennsylvania," and "Appalachian Trail."

The Appalachian Trail—where had I heard that name before? Then I remembered—I'd read an article about it in a Boy Scout magazine a few years before. Suddenly interested, I listened intently as Ray told of hiking the Pennsylvania section of the Appalachian Trail. It was an exciting account of mountain climbing and wilderness adventure.

"Fantastic experience," he said. "At one trail town where I stopped, I was even given a royal welcome by the mayor!"

Unfortunately, I could listen to only about five minutes of Ray's story before the bell rang and we had to return to our seats. But that was enough. I was smitten. As I slid into my seat, I vowed that someday I would hike the Appalachian Trail.

The seed had been planted.

Chapter 2

Decision Determines Destiny

> I will instruct you and teach you in the way you should go.
> —Psalm 32:8

Epiphanies are strange things. They burst into our lives when we least expect them.

One epiphany overpowered me in 1990, in a little Baptist church nestled in the hills of western Pennsylvania. As the visiting missionary, I just had presented a report to the congregation of our ministry in France. After the meeting, I chatted with some of the members and then stepped into the foyer of the old church. There, tacked on the wall, was the catalyst of my epiphany: a poster that riveted my attention and pulled me into a new experience and a new mission field.

The poster showed two men jogging up a steep mountain road. White birches and green spruce lined both sides of the narrow, winding blacktop. The two men wore running shorts, t-shirts, and wool stocking caps. Looking at their taut leg muscles, which testified to the strenuousness of their run, I could imagine their exhaustion. Despite the runners' obvious struggle—or perhaps because of it—the picture had adventure painted all over it.

As a jogger attracted to reasonable challenges, I was fascinated by the poster—but even more so by its caption: "With trust in God, let us venture beyond our limits."

As I stood there pondering both words and photo, I realized that together they presented one of the clearest pictures of faith I had ever seen. Trust . . . venture . . . beyond our limits. I was strangely stirred. This poster depicted faith in action: stepping out, attempting something for God beyond our capacity, while accepting the hardships and the potential risks involved.

It stirred me because I'd been struggling with an issue, a "mission impossible" gnawing the outer edges of my subconscious that I couldn't shake. And it was growing into a conviction that God was calling me to hike the Appalachian Trail as a witness for Him. Such an idea was, of course, ridiculous. Was I out of my mind? Sure, hiking the legendary trail sounded exciting, but at the same time, impossible. Hiking two-thousand miles through the wilderness, from Georgia to Maine, with a heavy pack on my back? Forget it. Besides, I knew little about the world of long-distance hiking. The men and women who did that sort of thing were a breed apart, as different from me as the people who walked on the moon. Doubts filled my mind and heart. How could I ever crack their culture and communicate with Appalachian Trail hikers, let alone hike beside them? And what about my fear of heights and my abysmal sense of direction?

As I stood gazing at the poster, Jack, the pastor of the church, walked into the foyer. He said, "Interesting picture, isn't it?"

"Sure is," I replied, and went on to explain why I was taken by the image and its message.

Pastor Jack made no further comment, but to my surprise, several weeks later, I received the poster in the mail. I wondered if Pastor Jack's unexpected gesture was a signal from heaven. I wanted to know if my strange impulses about hiking the Appalachian Trail were really from God. Life is too short to waste it on journeys to nowhere. I needed answers, so I pinned the poster to the wall of my study and began praying that the Lord would give me some solid direction.

While I waited, I read books to learn more about the Appalachian Trail and discovered much of its rich history. The trail was the brain-child of Benton McKaye, who had a vision for the trail that would span fourteen states as he meditated high in a tree on Vermont's Stratton Mountain in 1920. Eventually, after sharing his vision with others, the Appalachian Trail was built and officially opened to the public in 1937. The popularity of the AT, as it is affectionately called, grew with the passing years. Today it is a national icon, and approximately four million enthusiasts hike some portion of the AT each year.

Author Paul Hemphill wrote in his book *Me And the Boy* (Ballantine Books, 1986, p. 12):

> The Appalachian Trail is Yankee Stadium and the Rose Bowl
> and the Kentucky Derby and the Grand Ole Opry . . .

What had been one man's dream had captured the imagination of America.

Although I enjoyed my background reading, I still resisted the idea of hiking the AT because I knew it was beyond my capabilities. I had hiked in the mountains on occasion, but never for more than a day or two. Any attempt on my part to walk from Georgia to Maine would be a huge venture of faith. I questioned my ability to trust God that much. I was, after all, fifty-eight years old—not exactly the prime age for climbing mountains and plunging into the wilderness.

I also considered the difficulties I would encounter by trying to juggle long-distance hiking with my career as a missionary in France. My wife and I had served in France as church planters for more than thirty years, and we had a passion for that beautiful but spiritually dark country. I did not want to shortchange that mission in any way.

As for the physical endurance that hiking would demand, I had a few things going for me. Having been a jogger since my thirties and having run half-a-dozen marathons, I thought—perhaps naively—that my legs would be equal to the challenge. Added to this was my love for camping that dated back to my scouting days.

Then there was that mystical something about forests and the out-of-doors that I couldn't explain. I have an inborn affinity with nature and a longing for the wilderness; my earliest memories are of the created world. One spring morning when I was three, I discovered a rosebush in our backyard. The roses were covered with diamond-like beads of dew. My three-year-old lungs breathed in the fragrance, while my wide eyes feasted on the rich red and pink shades of beauty. A whole new world had opened to me, and from that moment, I was hooked on nature.

Then at five, exhausted after a summer's day of play, I lay in the cool of the evening on the grassy slope next to our home and looked up at the panorama of clouds in the sky above me. Though I had little understanding of God at the time, I sensed something special about that sky. My childish mind asked, "How can that sky be so beautiful and my life so unhappy?" I felt there was a reason for clouds and trees and flowers, and I wanted to understand that reason. Later, my conversion to Christ at age eleven gave me an entirely new comprehension of nature and deepened my love for the created world. Now I wanted to know more. I wanted to explore the forests and the mountains.

Yet, even greater than my passion for the out-of-doors was my burden to share the gospel of Christ with the throngs of people, especially young people, who each year hike the Appalachian Trail. In spite of my trepidation about the unknown wilderness and other dangers, my excitement at the challenge of witnessing to AT hikers grew, and I was now ready to undertake that mission for God.

After much prayer, I decided to follow my instincts. I always had heard that God could better guide the Christian who was moving than the Christian who was standing still. I would take the first step: join those two joggers in the poster struggling up that steep hill. I would venture beyond my limits, with trust in God, and see what happened. Maybe this was something for which God had been preparing me—for a very long time.

The Appalachian Trail

1992
30.7 miles hiked

Chapter 3

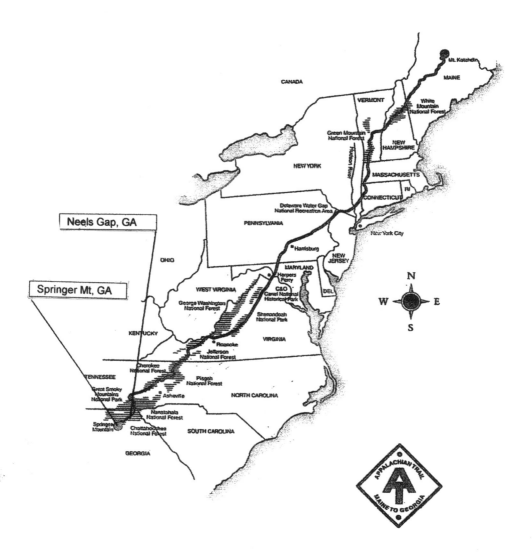

One Small Step for Man

Go into all the world and preach the gospel.

—Mark 16:15

Springer Mountain to Neels Gap

September 7, 1992: forty years, almost to the day, since I'd heard Ray's description of the Appalachian Trail in my high school homeroom . . . forty years since the desire to hike the trail had taken root in my spirit.

I stood at the foot of Springer Mountain, Georgia, at the beginning of the eight-mile approach trail that would lead me to the summit of Springer Mountain and the starting point of the fabled Appalachian Trail. This would be a trial run, a section hike of just four days, covering 30.7 miles. As a card-carrying "incrementalist," I like to take life one step at a time.

Although I hardly could contain my excitement, the excitement was nonetheless tempered by uncertainty, even fear, of the unknown. I was not at all sure I could do this, nor even dead certain that this was God's will.

I'd arrived early that morning at Amicalola State Park in northwest Georgia in a blue Jeep Wrangler driven by Charlie Shannon, my wife's twenty-four-year-old cousin. Hearing that I was going to hike the AT, Charlie had jumped into his Jeep and driven from Mississippi to join me, arriving late the night before.

Although I was happy to have Charlie's company, his presence made me a little edgy. Did I really want a witness with me if I bombed on the trail and had to turn back? Increasing my nervousness was the biting cold that had met us when we arrived at Amicalola. Not having expected frigid weather in Georgia in September, I hadn't even packed gloves.

Now the moment of reality had arrived—where the hiking boots hit the turf. Shouldering our heavy backpacks, Charlie and I took our first steps on the approach trail, and I thought, "One small step for man . . ." We were immediately engulfed by the woods. I felt the exhilaration of being in the wilderness, of at last following in the footsteps of those sturdy pioneer thru-hikers, four or five thousand of them, who had blazed the entire Appalachian Trail before me in decades past. Although I was only section hiking now, I felt privileged to be in their company.

These lofty thoughts were soon dissipated by the weight of my forty-eight-pound backpack. Somehow it hadn't felt this heavy in my in-laws' living room back in Ohio. The straps of my pack bit into my shoulders, and I felt the painful pull of gravity as I never had before. I groaned, *"Am I carrying cement or what?"*

Thirty minutes later, when we stopped for a break, the relief was so great that I felt like I was in heaven. Like most novice backpackers, I was carrying ten pounds too much. That revelation would not come to me until many miles down the trail. For now, I only could clench my teeth and bear it.

Three hours and numerous breaks later, Charlie and I finally reached the summit of Springer Mountain. The first taste of triumph! Giddy, I planted my feet at last on the sacred starting point of the whole Appalachian Trail. Charlie and I stood there, savoring the moment and looking out over the inspiring panorama from Springer. As had thousands before us, we had our photo taken beside the handsome bronze plaque with the image of an intrepid hiker engraved on it. Our spirits merged with the bronze hiker and his look of dogged determination—something that by then I was fully convinced was what we were going to need. Big time!

We began following the two-inch white blazes on trees that marked the trail. Not far from the bronze plaque, we came across, of all things, a metal mailbox. I turned to Charlie. "Is there really a postal service on the AT?"

Looking inside the box, we found not mail, but a spiral notebook used for recording the comings and goings of hikers, as well as their impressions, thoughts, and dreams. There were also messages for other hikers. This notebook-register was our first encounter with a unique system of communication that is an integral part of the trail experience.

After writing our names and a short note, I returned the notebook to the metal box. Then I noticed something else: a typed letter addressed to hikers, written by the parents of a young hiker named Mike. He had died of cancer before he could complete his thru-hike of the AT. Out of love for their son, they had sprinkled his ashes on the trail on his 33rd birthday. It read:

> Our hope is that this year's hikers will pick up our son's ashes on their boots, and carry them all the way to Mount Katahdin in Maine, the coveted destination that our son wanted to reach but never did because his life was cut short.

As a father of three sons, I was greatly moved by the grief of those dear parents and deeply touched by the love expressed in their gesture. Yet, I wished there was some mention of faith in the letter—some assurance that their son was in heaven because he had trusted Christ. I wished I could have met Mike and talked to him about eternity. Then I remembered that all of the hikers I would meet on the AT would someday die, and I resolved with God's help to share the gospel with as many of them as I could, before it was too late.

In spite of our age difference, Charlie, my hiking partner, and I got along well. Charlie—tall, handsome, and intelligent—talked about becoming an FBI agent some day. I was confident he would do well in whatever career he decided to pursue.

Things had not always been easy for Charlie. Tragedy broke into his life when he was eight. His dad, while returning from a business trip in a company plane, was killed when the plane crashed. The loss of a father could devastate a boy. Although I never knew how Charlie had handled his father's death sixteen years before, I now hoped I'd have the opportunity to see how he was doing emotionally and spiritually.

That opportunity came during our second night out as we sat in front of an after-supper campfire. It wasn't an ideal setting: the damp firewood smoked and floated in the air around us, and there was the distinct odor of a dead animal rotting somewhere nearby. (I later discovered a dead rabbit and gave him a proper burial.)

As we talked that evening, we fell into the subject of the Christian life. "How's it going with you spiritually, Charlie?" I asked.

"Could be better," he replied. "I need to work on my walk with God."

He had accepted Christ when he was a boy, but now his faith was not strong. I encouraged Charlie to center his life in God's will and get into God's Word daily. It was a simple discussion, but one I hoped the Lord would use somehow in Charlie's life.

On the fourth and last day of our hike, we reached Blood Mountain, Georgia's highest summit. By now, Charlie was hiking well ahead of me. "Blood Mountain," I mused. "What a name for a mountain!" I had read of the battle between Creek and Cherokee Indians that had taken place there. It was a conflict so violent that the ground and rocks were stained with blood.

As I hiked the top of the mountain, I thought of the stark contrast between that story and the splendid vista stretched out before me. How in all this beauty could people do such things? I knew the answer from reading the Bible: because of sin, this is the condition of men's hearts everywhere and in every period of history.

Suddenly, I came on a stone hiker's shelter. By then, fog had moved in, and it was so thick that I almost passed the shelter without seeing it. Stone shelters are rare on the trail, and this one, built in 1934, was rumored to have housed a bear one winter. I decided to check out the place.

When I stepped inside the shelter and saw its condition, I immediately believed the bear story. Although the interior was dark, I could see a lot of trash scattered around. As my eyes adjusted to the darkness, I noticed two young men sitting by a fireplace in which the fire had died and only cold ashes remained. The dimness, along with the disorder and cold, made a gloomy setting.

"How's it going, guys?" I asked. The men returned my greeting, and we exchanged a few words of conversation about the trail and other generalities. As I talked with the two hikers, I remembered that I had two gospel tracts in my shirt pocket. In spite of my exhaustion, aches, and pains, the hike had been a great experience, but I was troubled by one thing: I had not talked to one unsaved person about Christ. I was disappointed. This was the chief reason for my hiking the AT. However, not one opportunity for witnessing had presented itself.

Thankful for this opportunity, I took the two tracts from my pocket and gave them to the two fellows, telling them the tracts contained an important message from the Bible. They accepted my offer readily, and I went on my way.

Hiking down the north side of Blood Mountain was much easier than climbing up. Although the fog was still thick in some places, I discerned an unusual rock formation. Then I remembered that I had seen those very rocks in a *National Geographic* article about the AT. Delighted by my find, I took a photo of the spot and continued my descent.

When I finally emerged from the fog, I was only a quarter of a mile from our destination, Neels Gap. A voice called from behind me, and I turned around to see a well-built young man with a heavy pack on his back. He was accompanied by a German shepherd carrying a heavy pack on its back. The young man was waving a paper in his hand. I then recognized him as one of the hikers I had met at the stone shelter on Blood Mountain—one to whom I had given a tract.

"I read this, and want to talk to you about it," the young man said, holding up the tract. He introduced himself as John Clark, a student at the University of Georgia. I replied that I'd be happy to talk with him. Keeping my eye on the German shepherd, I suggested we take off our packs and sit on the grassy slope next to the trail.

"I'm a Methodist," the young man confided when we sat down, "but I have a lot of doubts." For about twenty minutes we discussed faith and God's plan of salvation. I shared with John my testimony and urged him to make sure he truly had put his trust in Christ. He thanked me and said he would think about what I'd said.

The university student and his German shepherd moved on down the trail. I continued at my slower pace, with a happy heart. I believed the Lord had just given me the confirmation I needed. I could be a witness for Him on the Appalachian Trail. It was the answer to my prayer and the start of 2,000 miles of making Christ known to hikers. I had ventured beyond my limits, and God had honored that step of faith. I was jubilant.

Minutes later, I arrived at Neels Gap, where a car shuttled Charlie and me back to his parked Jeep at Amicalola Park. After four days and thirty miles of backpacking strain and fatigue, it felt rapturous to be swept along in a powered vehicle. I relaxed in the soft comfort of a cushioned car seat and thought of my next hike . . . and beyond—on the Appalachian Trail.

The Appalachian Trail

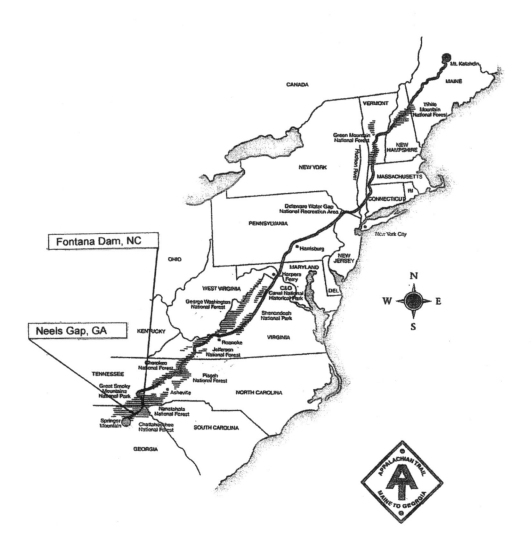

Fontana Dam, NC

Neels Gap, GA

Chapter 4

Albert Mountain and Other Spiritual Encounters

Is there anything too hard for the Lord?

—Genesis 18:14

Neels Gap, Georgia, to Winding Stair Gap, North Carolina

May 15, 1994: "Y'all have a good hike now." With these words, our shuttle driver, Charlie Watts, deposited my youngest son, Mark, and me at Neels Gap, Georgia, where I had finished my first section hike on the Appalachian Trail two years earlier. My wife and I were in the US on a three-month furlough from France, and between missionary meetings, I was sandwiching in an eleven-day hike on the AT.

I was pleased that Mark, recently graduated from Messiah College in Pennsylvania, had accepted my invitation to hike the next section with me. I felt that physically he would be up to the challenge. In high school he had been captain of the soccer team, and in college, an outstanding runner, so speedy that he had qualified to run in the Penn Relays in Philadelphia.

While Mark and I hiked the AT, my wife, Babs, would spend time with her parents in Ohio. We had prayed together about this venture, and she was on board. I place a high value on my wife's opinion; her agreeing that this mission was of God was critical in my decision to hike the trail. And I knew that her help would be invaluable were I ever to reach Maine.

"Just don't get bitten by a snake," she'd said.

Mark and I had driven all night from Pennsylvania to Fontana Dam, about 120 miles north of Neels Gap, in his ancient LeBaron. Then Charlie Watts, our shuttle person, picked us up at the parking lot of Fontana Dam. Having survived the drive, we would now, if all went well, hike the 120 miles from Neels Gap to Fontana Dam and the parked LeBaron.

I liked Charlie Watts from the first moment. He was a smiling North Carolinian in his fifties, with a deep voice and a deep-South accent to match. As we cruised through the mountains in his van toward Neels Gap, Charlie regaled us with stories about his life. He had been saved as a boy but had later wandered away from God. It took the near-death of his son in an auto accident and the serious illness of his grand-daughter to awaken Charlie and bring him to repentance and spiritual restoration. Now Charlie was serving the Lord by sharing his faith and planting churches in his area of North Carolina.

"We got a church in every holler," he announced proudly over the roar of the motor.

Charlie's testimony was just what I needed as we prepared to launch this second AT expedition. His changed life was a reminder that nothing is too hard for the Lord.

That encouragement was put to the test as my son and I left Neels Gap and headed north on the trail. The rain came—softly at first and then harder. At the end of a mile, even wearing our ponchos, Mark and I were uncomfortably wet.

At 7:00 p.m., we came upon a rustic campsite and decided to spend the night there. We put up my small Eureka tent in the rain and crawled in, wet packs and all. Stripping off wet t-shirts and pants, we struggled into humid sleeping bags. Supper was not even mentioned as we quickly fell asleep. This was not the euphoric beginning I had envisioned for our hike, but it would have to do.

I awoke the next morning before 6:00 to humidity so heavy that it seemed to wrap itself around us in the tent. Unzipping the door a couple of inches, I peered out and saw a world enveloped in fog. Thankfully, the rain had stopped, but everything looked dark and uninviting. Water dripped from every tree, bush, and blade of grass.

As the leader of this expedition, I felt I had to do something, so I eased myself out of my sleeping bag and, trying not to awaken my son, struggled into dry clothes and damp boots. I then crept out of the tent. Once outside, there was only one thing I could do in the semi-darkness: pray. While Mark slept, I paced the length of our small campsite, praying, "Lord, help us get through this first day of our hike."

Twenty minutes later, I heard Mark moving around in the tent. While he was dressing, I started breakfast. My first job was to fire up my stove, but when I looked for my matches, I couldn't find them. I searched through my pack twice, but they weren't there.

"Try mine," Mark said, tossing his matches, but they were wet from the rain, useless. No matches meant no hot tea, no hot oatmeal, no hot anything. I was devastated. What could I have done with the matches? How do you survive in the wilderness without a fire?

After a cold breakfast of granola and bagels, we glumly prepared to leave. As I zipped up my pack, I remembered that I had put the matches in a secret pocket of my backpack to keep them dry. With a whoop of relief, I told Mark and praised the Lord for answering my cry of distress. God was with us. We would survive in spite of my forgetfulness and disorganization. With lifted spirits, we hoisted our packs and started down the trail.

Thirty minutes later the fog lifted, and the sun came out bright and glorious, transforming our whole world. A once miserable day was now a perfect one for hiking. Overhead were sun and blue skies and fleeting clouds; and around us, ferns, tall grass, and trees were swaying in the wind. The cool breeze caressed my face and tousled my hair. Following a couple of paces behind my son, I reveled in the glory of God's world. Something within me said that this was where I belonged, that God had created me to hike the Appalachian Trail.

Mark and I covered fifteen miles that day—too much for the first day, but we were on a roll. The sun was still high when we arrived at a shelter. We draped our clothes and tent, still wet from the day before, over nearby bushes to dry. Inside the sunbathed, three-sided shelter, I rolled out my sleeping bag and sat on it, resting my back against the shelter wall. My whole body tingled with a pleasant fatigue as I looked out on the lush green of the forest in front of the shelter. A fabulous feeling of well-being overcame me. "This must be the nearest thing to heaven on earth," I said to myself. Seldom had I ever felt such inner peace and satisfaction.

Not all of our experiences were, of course, so satisfying. On Tray Mountain the next night, we were introduced to the denizens of the AT shelters—mice! They had taken over Tray Shelter, and as soon as flashlights were turned off and candles snuffed, the little creatures came out for their nightly raids.

We thought the mice would not be a problem because our packs were off the ground, free-hanging on hooks overhead. Not a chance. These mice could have qualified for the Olympics! No leap was too difficult for them. We had been dozing only an hour when Mark yelled out, "There's a spider on me!" As it turned out, the "spider" was an athletic mouse that had leaped from an overhead rafter and landed on Mark's head. That experience was a bit out of our comfort zone, but eventually we and our shelter mates returned to sleep—albeit, a somewhat troubled sleep.

In the spring, the AT blossoms with great numbers of hikers, most of them normal people looking for adventure and contact with nature. There were a few along our journey, however, who were harder to categorize. One young couple, Rob Roy—who had long hair—and Judy—who wore riding breeches—seemed uncomfortable on the trail and not quite sure why they were there. When I offered Judy a gospel tract titled "Where will you spend eternity?" she accepted it reluctantly. I assumed she had no interest in spiritual matters, even with reminders of the Creator all around her, but I prayed that she might read the message I had given her.

THE HEADLESS HIKER

Hands down, the strangest person we met on the trail was a hiker-biker, whom we ran into just before we arrived at Carter Shelter. We were eager to reach Carter because it was rumored that a trail maintainer stocked cold drinks behind the shelter. We wanted to find out if the rumor was true.

As we approached Carter Shelter, I noticed a strange sight directly in front of us: a hiker who appeared to be headless! As we got closer, I realized the hiker did indeed have a head, but his pack was piled so high with gear that his head was not visible. We arrived at the shelter at the same time. The hiker, a bearded man in his forties with the overhanging stomach of someone who did not hike a great deal, was limping, and as soon as he sat down on the floor of the shelter, he began cursing loudly about a twisted ankle.

We and several others stood in stunned silence. In an effort to calm the man I said, "How about if I pray for your ankle?"

To my amazement, at the mention of prayer, the man stopped cursing and began quoting Scripture and singing hymns. Then he told us that his trail name was "Hiker-Biker" and he had crossed the US nine times on his motorcycle. He had been baptized a Catholic, later became a Baptist, and while biking across Colorado, had joined some sect that worshiped God's name rather than God himself.

My efforts to talk to Hiker-Biker about the gospel were to no avail. He continued ranting. Finally, out of sheer frustration, I bowed my head and prayed aloud for his twisted ankle and asked God to, above all, move in his life and calm his soul.

We left Hiker-Biker sitting at the shelter, the rumored soft drinks forgotten. I wish I could say we helped the man, but I'm afraid we did not. The encounter was unnerving, but perhaps not without value. If nothing else, it was a reminder to me that in my efforts to witness to hikers, I would face spiritual battles. My AT hike would not be a cakewalk.

The experience with Hiker-Biker was followed by a challenge of a different kind: Albert Mountain. I had read intimidating descriptions of the climb up Albert Mountain. One source called it "fabled," another referred to it as "notorious." According to one report, it would take an agonizing hour to scale Albert Mountain, and I wondered if this climb would be too much for me—my Waterloo. I was not looking forward to Albert Mountain.

We arrived at Albert in the heat of the day. "Three-tenths of a mile and straight up," the guidebook said. Was I ready for this—especially with a heavy pack on my back? I drank generous swigs of water at the bottom of Albert, trying to delay the inevitable. Finally, summoning my courage and feeling like General Eisenhower announcing the Normandy invasion to his troops, I said to Mark, "Well, let's go."

We began climbing. In minutes, to our surprise, we discovered that by grasping tree roots sticking out here and there, we could pull ourselves up. At the halfway point, Mark and I were joking. We actually were having fun. When we reached the top of Albert, I looked at my watch and announced, "Twenty-five minutes." The climb had taken us not an agonizing hour but a fun-filled twenty-five minutes! What I had been dreading turned out to be a rewarding experience. I wondered how many other times in my life I had backed away from intimidating challenges and consequently missed some great blessings, all because I was afraid. I would remember Albert Mountain the next time I wanted to avoid a challenge.

Mark and I were running out of food, which is an ever-present problem for all hungry backpackers, so we decided to hit the off-trail Rainbow Campground to resupply and take a shower. We were walking down a dirt road toward the camp when a van pulled alongside of us and a voice inside asked, "Want a ride?"

We turned and saw that it was Bob, a fiftyish man hiking the AT with his college-age daughter, Mickey. We had bumped into them several times on the trail and had enjoyed some good conversations. As a father-son team, we felt a certain kinship with this father-daughter team.

Their mode of travel was different from ours, as they used two vehicles parked at each end of a section. This allowed them to stay in motels, essentially making them day hikers.

We gladly accepted the offer of a ride, and I got in the front seat next to Bob. Although it was only a short drive to the campground, Bob made a wrong turn, and we ended up going six miles out of our way.

This mistake seemed to me a God-given opportunity to talk to Bob about the Lord. Plunging right in, I asked him if he had thought about eternity and if he felt ready to meet the Lord after this life. He replied that because his father had been a minister he knew a lot about religion and was doing all he could to help people.

I told Bob that was commendable but that being right with God involves a personal relationship with Christ through acknowledging our sin and asking Him to be our Savior. I followed that up with my own testimony of salvation. At that, he lapsed into silence, and a few moments later, we arrived at Rainbow Campground. I hoped I hadn't come on too strong with Bob, but I felt right in seizing the opportunity, and I believed the Lord would use my witness in spite of any gaffes on my part.

At Rainbow Campground, Mark and I took showers—our first in six days—and then devoured a twelve-inch Taco Pizza and resupplied with food for the trail. Buddy, the campground owner, kindly shuttled us back to the trail. On the ride, I mentioned our encounter with Hiker-Biker and the possibility that he might show up at the campground. A frightened look came over Buddy's face. I guessed he'd dealt with problem hikers in the past and was not looking forward to any more.

VOICES IN THE NIGHT

Saturday evening we finished our sixth day on the trail. Just beyond Winding Stair Gap, we camped for the night at a beautiful site beside a rushing mountain stream. For backpackers, it didn't get any better than this. The place could have been a photo opportunity for *Backpacker Magazine*. While Mark set up the tent, I made a fire. Our campsite was soon swallowed up by darkness, our only light from the burning logs.

As we sat gazing at the fire, I said, "I hear voices, moaning voices."

"Yeah, I hear 'em, too," Mark replied.

They were definitely human voices; although, we couldn't understand the words and couldn't determine where they were coming from. Were they spirits of long-departed Native Americans who still roamed the forests? It was downright spooky. Mystified, we doused the fire and retreated to our tent for the night.

The next morning brought an answer. We learned from a hiker that a group of Boy Scouts had been camping a half-mile upstream. Evidently, the water had carried the sound of their voices downstream to our campsite. I'd heard of this phenomenon before, and I was glad to know we hadn't imagined things the previous night.

Later, as I thought about the spooky incident, I concluded that it was a metaphor of my fears about the wilderness. Most of those fears were turning out to be just "phantoms." Experience and a stronger trust in the Lord were helping me to feel at home in the wilderness.

Chapter 5

On a Clear Day You Can See Forever

I will lift up my eyes to the hills.

—Psalm 121:1

Winding Stair Gap to Fontana Dam, North Carolina

May 22, day seven, we were struggling up really big mountains. This was the heart of the Great Smoky Mountains. The climb up Siler's Bald was especially gut-wrenching. Hiking the Appalachian Trail was the most exhausting thing I had ever done, harder even than running marathons. I swam in sweat with every step I took. Every item of clothing I wore, including my socks, was drenched. My colored t-shirt was blotched with white circles from the salt that poured from my perspiring body. Countless times, I questioned my sanity in even attempting to climb such impossible peaks. "Climb Every Mountain"—yeah, right. (For the record, there are 650 mountains on the AT.) Dozens of times a day, every part of my body cried out to quit the trail and go home.

Especially maddening were the "mirage summits" of the mountains Mark and I climbed, which always appeared to be just over the next rise but almost never were. Like the man dying of thirst in the desert, who keeps seeing pools of cool, clear water, I kept seeing mountain summits that evaporated before my eyes. Adding to my torment was the deadweight of my pack, which felt like a load of bricks instead of hiking gear. The pull on my shoulders was pure torture. I hated gravity. I wanted to strangle Isaac Newton.

But as difficult as the physical strain was, the emotional drain was even worse. The fatigue wreaked havoc on our emotions. It hit Mark first, and he was in a down mood as we ended the first week of our hike. We talked little that seventh day on the trail.

During the years Mark and I had been separated—first during his three years at Black Forest Academy in Germany while Babs and I served in France, and then during his years in college in the States—I had forgotten about his moody side. Like his father, he has a poetic personality that is subject to mood swings. I thought of my own battles at his age with emotional ups and downs. I was in my forties before I got a handle on them, and once in a while, I still have a day when I battle gloom and discouragement. We both were learning that hiking the AT had a way of exposing the raw edges of our emotional weaknesses. Maybe getting those weaknesses out in the open would help us deal with them.

Another source of tension was that Mark—and my other two sons—and I never had discussed was my weaknesses as a father. While my three sons were growing up, I probably considered myself a cut above the average dad. For example, I usually read them a bedtime Bible story, and each summer we went camping together for a week or ten days. But with the passing years, the tensions with my sons made my failings more apparent.

Because my work as a missionary involved only occasional trips from home, I was not an absent father in the sense that I traveled a lot. But I was so involved in our ministry to the French that I was absent in spirit. And frankly, my job of mentoring my sons had been a dismal failure. My parents' divorce had deprived me of a father's direction in my life, and this weakness was reflected in my failure to properly train my sons. Some fathers have a gift for mentoring their sons. I did not. Mentoring was not even on my mind. As my sons were growing up, I didn't do enough to involve them in our missionary work or give them skills for life.

Added to this was a life that centered too much on me. I was self-absorbed in many ways. My love for reading kept my nose in a book when I should have been interacting with my sons. Add to that all the demands of a missionary-pastor. When I wasn't working, I was out jogging for miles by myself, just to have some time alone. I called my jogs my "mini-vacations."

I also had a great passion for prayer. I spent hours, even days, in personal prayer retreats. I didn't regret this, but later I understood that it created a chasm between my sons and me. Although I was sure my sons loved me, I felt a simmering resentment. I never had dealt with it. I wondered how that problem would play out on the trail with my youngest son, hiking and being together twenty-four hours a day. I was already learning that long-distance hiking has a way of exposing relational problems. I also was becoming convinced that hiking together while facing the same challenges, sharing the same aches and pains, and discussing life's issues, was a wonderful way of healing, and even cementing, relationships.

At Cold Springs Shelter on day eight, we met three male hikers, two large Labrador retriever dogs, and a short and perky blonde named Heather, who seemed to be in charge of both hikers and dogs. One of the Labs was called "Walden," after Thoreau's famous pond. Walden was a friendly dog, so friendly that he slept next to me in the shelter that night, and not surprisingly, I awoke the next morning with a dozen flea bites on my upper body. This was not exactly my idea of trail fellowship.

While eating my Grape Nuts that morning, I noticed one of the three men reading a book called *Narcotics Anonymous*. This confirmed what I'd already suspected: the group was part of a drug rehabilitation program, and Heather was their leader. I wasn't sure how the dogs fit in, but I was learning that the AT has many uses and meets many needs.

Descending Copper Ridge Bald, Mark and I discussed Walden Pond, Thoreau's life, and his sometimes quirky ideas. Then we moved on to the English poet Lord Byron and his amazing talents and wasted life. If only Byron, we concluded, had renounced his decadent ways and turned to Christ, what a difference it would have made for him and the world.

Then, as men will do, we got on to the subject of sex. "How did you handle things when you were young?" Mark asked.

What a thorny question for a father! I replied, "I wasn't especially proud of my behavior in that area when I was in high school. There are things I wish I could go back and change. But one thing that kept me from moral disaster was hearing my mother, your grandmother, praying for me in her bedroom when I came home at night. I'll thank God forever for my mother and her prayers."

Mark seemed content with my response to his question, and he knew that I was praying daily for him.

Our discussions were not always easy, but again, I was realizing that hiking the AT together had given our relationship a rare opportunity to grow and deepen. In perhaps no other setting would this change have been as readily possible, and I concluded that hiking the AT allows fathers and sons to bond in an unusual way.

THE ONE-HUNDRED-MILE MARK

We were now moving down the mountain toward the trail town of Wesser, North Carolina. I was surprised and delighted to see white azaleas blooming as we reached the lower, warmer altitudes. Our "tunnel of green" (as hikers refer to the over-arching trees and bushes) suddenly became a tunnel of white, and the beauty and aroma of the azaleas put us in a good mood as we neared Wesser.

Adding to my satisfaction was discovering that I had now hiked 100 miles on the Appalachian Trail, a significant milestone for me. I was still 2,000 miles from Katahdin, but having put that first 100 miles behind me brightened my hope that I would one day reach Maine.

Hiking into Wesser the morning of May 24, we had one all-consuming interest—food! Burning five or six thousand calories a day leaves a huge hollow in a hiker's stomach. Although we weren't really starving, we certainly felt as if we were. Visions of thick pancakes, maple syrup, fried eggs, and link sausage danced in our minds.

Fortunately, we didn't have to wait long to satisfy our hunger. The Riverfront Restaurant, sitting on the wild Nantahala River, is one of the first places you meet when you hike into Wesser. We left our packs outside the restaurant, positioned where we could keep our eyes on them from inside the restaurant by looking through the picture window. Hikers learn never to let their packs out of sight. The pack is their lifeline to survival.

We ordered a huge breakfast and then settled back to read the newspaper while we waited for our food. Mark took the sports pages, groaning as he read that his favorite teams—the Phoenix Suns and Chicago Bulls—had lost their games. The good news was that Pete Sampras had qualified for the finals in the French Open tennis tournament. I read about Jackie Onassis's death and burial, Rep. Dan "Rosty" Rostenkowski's indictment, and the Clinton Health Care plan that was near death.

Our breakfast arrived, and we dug in with gusto. It was delicious—at least at first. But by the end of the meal, I was feeling queasy, and it looked as if Mark did too. All that rich food was a shock to our systems after so many days living a Spartan regime in the wilderness. We were learning that rich is not always better.

After breakfast, I had another shock when I went to the nearby public restroom to wash my face and shave and was confronted by the sight in the mirror. Who was that person looking back at me? It could not be the Rev. Charles Anderson! The man in the mirror had baggy eyes, his right eye was almost swollen shut from an insect bite, and he had a three-day-old beard. That was not me in the mirror. It was a graying, punch-drunk prizefighter with a tan. It was not the kind of person you wanted to meet in a dark alley. No wonder people in town had looked askance at me. Fortunately, after washing my face, shaving, and combing my hair, I once again resembled a member of the human race.

We found a pay phone and called home. Hearing Babs' voice brought me out of my world of conquering mountains and following little white blazes through the woods. My wilderness life was completely foreign to her, and her fast-paced civilized world sounded strangely unfamiliar to me. My mind had trouble adjusting to the events she described, but I made a huge effort and succeeded, at least in a measure, in answering my wife's questions: "Yes, we can take a week to present missions at a junior-high Christian camp on Lake Erie in July. It would be OK to speak to a supporting church in southern Ohio the Sunday after that.

It will be wonderful to hear about Mark's job interview when he gets back."

My wife had known we were still alive because she had called Rainbow Springs Campground and was told that two hikers answering to our description had passed through. Expressing my love to my wife, I returned the phone to its cradle and slipped back into my world of long-distance hiking through the wilderness.

It was all uphill from Wesser, and our backs groaned under the weight of the food we'd purchased in town. Our next stop was Sassafras Shelter, which we reached in the late afternoon. Twenty-four years before, Ed Garvey, thru-hiker and well-known author of several books on the AT, described this same shelter as so depressing that he had decided not to stay there. Nothing had changed in the intervening years. Sassafras still looked dirty and depressing, with a sizable erosion ditch passing in front of it. The place was the picture of desolation.

Looking back, I'm not surprised that my son and I had our most serious disagreement at this shelter. I had proposed that, because it was 4:30, we eat supper at Sassafras and then climb Mount Cheoah, directly to the north of us. Mark was dead set against that idea, and we locked horns on the issue. It was a silly matter to argue over, and I shouldn't have insisted on my way, but later events proved it to be a good decision. Mark remained angry, so we ate supper in silence and then packed quickly and headed up the mountain.

STORM ON THE MOUNTAIN

Forty-five minutes later, we arrived at the summit of Mount Cheoah. The guidebook had promised a beautiful vista, and a beautiful vista it was. In every direction we saw the surrounding mountains rising in an endless horizon. As we took in the stunning panorama stretched out before us, we forgot about our dispute.

A large meadow on Cheoah convinced us that we should camp on the summit for the night. What better campsite than one surrounded by majestic mountains? After Mark took some water and went behind some bushes for a sponge bath, I noticed storm clouds gathering in the sky and decided we needed to set up the tent.

I had just finished putting up the tent when the storm broke with fury. I grabbed our backpacks. Cutting short his bath, Mark ran over, and we dove into the tent. Thunder and lightning strikes were all around us.

Sitting on top of a mountain in the open is not the safest place during an electrical storm. We felt vulnerable, and over the roar of the wind and the claps of thunder, I yelled to my son, "I think we'd better pray," which we did. Then we counted the seconds between the lightning and thunder claps. They were only two or three seconds apart at first, but gradually, the lapses lengthened. And finally, after a scary twenty minutes, the thunder ceased, the rain stopped, the sun came out, and a wonderful calm settled on the mountain. Peace. It must have been like this, I thought, when Noah and the ark settled on Mount Ararat after the rain had stopped and the floodwaters had subsided. We felt the same thankfulness that Noah must have felt when that awesome storm was over.

I dug out my paperback book and started to read a few pages in the waning daylight. Lacing up his sneakers, Mark said he was going for a stroll. When a half hour had passed and the sun was setting, I decided to check on him. After walking only a short distance, I spotted him sitting on a rocky ledge that jutted out over a thousand-foot drop, gazing at a vast chain of Smoky Mountains that stretched to the very edges of eternity.

Sensing that he might be in some serious meditation and not wanting to disturb the sacredness of the moment, I silently retraced my steps to the tent. When Mark slipped into the tent later, it was night, and I was asleep.

The next morning as we hiked off the summit of Cheoah, I asked Mark, "What were you doing last evening?"

"Looking at the mountains, thinking about my life," he replied. "It brought a lot of things into focus. I realized how good God has been to me and all the privileges I've had. I was overwhelmed with gratitude."

Hearing my son's explanation swept away my fatigue and muscle strain. His mountaintop experience had been worth all the exhaustion and vanishing summits, and I felt a new bounce in my step.

On day nine, when we stopped for lunch at Brown Fort Shelter, who should show up but Judy of the riding breeches.

"Rob Roy and I have split," she announced. She was hiking alone now.

Knowing she was discouraged, I offered some words of comfort. Judy now seemed more humble and more open to spiritual things. Life's disappointments have a way of reminding us that we need God.

Day ten, Wednesday, May 25, was our next to last day on the trail. We reached Cody Gap and found a large campsite, which was ideal for our last night in the wilderness. No one else showed up, so we had it all to ourselves.

We were in a festive mood that last evening. Because I always needed newspaper to start my fires, Mark built the fire that night and proudly announced, "One match and no paper!" Then we combined our remaining two packages of cheddar cheese and pasta and sauce and created a tasty dish, worthy of our last supper together on the AT.

We spent our last evening in front of the fire talking about the hiking experience that was about to end, what it meant to us, and what we had learned about ourselves, God, and the wilderness. We both agreed that it had been satisfying. We talked until the fire died and our campsite became engulfed in darkness.

Although we didn't discuss our relationship, I felt that something had taken place and we were now communicating as man to man. Perhaps some of my past weaknesses as a father had been put to rest. In any case, more than ever before, I felt we were on the same team.

The next morning, day eleven, we were on the trail at 9:00, with only an easy ten-mile hike between us and Fontana Dam. After our lunch break, it started raining, just a drizzle at first, and then much heavier. For the last three miles, we slogged through a deep, dark forest in a tropical rain. Although the downpour was uncomfortable, I noticed, but not for the first time, that there is a mysterious beauty in a rainforest. Steam rises from the forest floor, and the pungent odors from rotting logs and vegetation smell like nothing else in this world.

We were finishing our hike as we began it—in the rain—but I was not unhappy in the least. I had enjoyed hiking through this enchanted forest. It seemed a great way for Mark and me to end our AT experience.

We reached Fontana Dam in early afternoon. As we crossed the parking lot to Mark's car, a brown van drove slowly by us, its tires spinning water. Through the rain-spattered windows, we saw the van's two occupants waving at us. As we waved back to Bob and Mickey, I felt a touch of sadness, knowing that we would never meet again on this earth. I prayed that someday our paths would cross again . . . in heaven.

We threw our wet packs into the trunk of Mark's car and changed into dry clothes. Then we climbed into the LeBaron and headed for Ohio, another section of my journey to Maine now history. The end of one adventure always seems to be the beginning of a new one, and already, I was looking forward to the adventures of the next hike.

The Appalachian Trail

1996
176.2 miles hiked

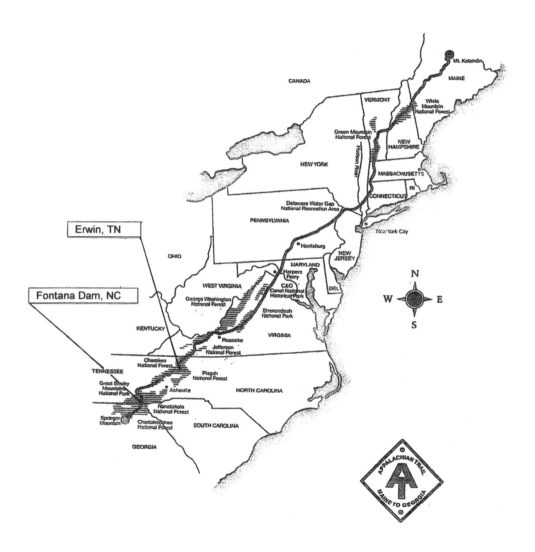

Chapter 6

Brave Heart and Bad Weather

Endure hardness as a good soldier of Jesus Christ.
—2 Timothy 2:3

Fontana Dam to New Found Gap, North Carolina

161.7 Miles Hiked

Two years had passed, and it was now 1996. In early April, my wife and I had said *au revoir* to France, our home and mission field for thirty-three years. Leaving our ministry and our many friends and coworkers there was hard on our emotions. We shed tears as we said "good-bye" to them. We would always love France and would return for visits whenever possible, but we felt our church-planting ministry there was completed. The three Baptist churches that God had raised up in Bordeaux had good leadership and were growing: mission accomplished.

On my mind as we flew across the Atlantic to the US was the new ministry to which God had called me on the Appalachian Trail. I looked forward to my AT mission and to new adventures in witnessing to hikers. Resettling in the US would allow more time for hiking larger sections of the AT.

After our return to Ohio, I had only a month to get ready for my next section hike, so I had to hustle. Long-distance hiking takes a surprising amount of preparation. There were weeks of meals to be planned, equipment to buy and try out, shuttles to be arranged, a tent to be sealed, and new boots to break in. At times the list seemed endless. For a couple of weeks, my hiking gear was spread all over the family room.

A challenge I continually worked on was reducing my pack weight. I learned to look at every piece of gear, no matter how large or small, and ask the question, "Do I really need this?" I repackaged food into feather-weight containers. I bought a postal scale and spent hours weighing each of the nearly one hundred pieces of gear I carried. Every ounce I shaved off my pack weight was cause for celebration. I became such a fanatic that I sawed off part of the handle of my toothbrush to make it lighter!

And of course, there is physical preparation as well, which, in my case, involved weeks of jogging and weight training. The goal I set was to feel comfortable after jogging for two hours.

One new feature of my hike was that I finally had decided on a trail name. After considering several possibilities, I chose the name "Onward!" I liked that title because it expressed not only the attitude I wanted on this hike but also my goal in life. "Onward!" became my hiker ID on the Appalachian Trail.

My eldest son, Chad, would be hiking with me this time, and I could tell he was excited about doing the AT. In his junior year at Cedarville College in Ohio, Chad had been drafted into the French Air Force and had served in a commando division as a paratrooper. That experience had sharpened his interest in adventure.

Chad drove his Jeep from Indiana to Ohio to pick me up, and from there, we drove to North Carolina. On the way there I encountered an old nemesis—anxiety. Questions swirled in my mind. Had I really packed the tent poles? Were my hiking boots in the trunk of the car? Did I have the bottle of propane gas for the stove? I was obsessed with the idea that I had forgotten something important and that my hike would be scuttled because I didn't have that piece of gear.

My fears evolved into a spiritual battle, stemming, I suspected, from my desire to witness for Christ on the trail. I said nothing to Chad about my inner battle, but recited Scripture and confessed my unbelief to the Lord. Finally, peace came. Although I would experience some anxiety during future hikes, with the Lord's help, the intensity and duration of my fears decreased.

We arrived at Newfound Gap, North Carolina, on May 12, 1996, and parked Chad's jeep. Once again, Charlie Watts was our shuttle driver to Fontana Dam, North Carolina, which would be our starting point. As I expected, we enjoyed another fine time of fellowship with Charlie on the drive to Fontana.

Having arrived in the late afternoon, we decided to spend the night at the Fontana "Hilton," the name given by hikers to AT shelters that are larger and more comfortable than the usual three-sided shelters. The spacious and well-built Fontana shelter richly deserved its distinguished title.

That afternoon, it was filled with excited thru-hikers chattering happily and congratulating each other for making it from Springer Mountain to Fontana Dam. With a dropout rate of ninety percent, however, very few of these hikers would reach Maine. But for the moment, they basked in their accomplishment, and I was happy for them.

Darkness fell as I wrote in my journal. The cold was creeping into our bodies, so we crawled into our sleeping bags. Charlie Watts had warned us that the temperature would drop to thirty-two degrees that night. Chad and I slept in our clothes to make sure we would be warm enough. It worked, and Chad admitted to feeling only slightly cold during the night.

As we ate breakfast the next morning, the sun came out bright and cheerful. Before leaving Fontana, we asked someone to take our photo as we stood by Fontana Lake with our packs on, smiling and ready for the challenge that lay ahead.

The weather was on good behavior during the first two days. Chad and I hiked along paths lined with wildflowers caressed by the sun. Spring was in the air, and we took many photos. Although we were having a good experience, I knew that the rosy scenario wouldn't last forever.

STRANDED AT SPENCE FIELD

Late afternoon on the second day, the weather turned cold and the rain arrived. Rain and cold together are the worst of all worlds for the hiker. We hiked ten miles to Spence Field Shelter and decided to hole up there. The shelter was large, and we would have stayed inside, but it was already crowded. We pitched our tent in the area around the shelter. At least a dozen other hikers were doing the same, so it looked like a backpackers' convention.

It rained hard all night. Our tent didn't leak, and we were thankful that the tent sealer was working. But in the morning, we felt the cold dampness and decided to retreat to the comfort of the shelter's cozy fire. Other tent dwellers with the same idea were now crowded into the shelter along with their gear. Though we appreciated the warmth generated by so many bodies, there was little room to move about.

Fortunately, Spence Field Shelter had an upper platform for sleeping, and Chad and I found just enough space on the platform to sit and prepare our breakfast. Using my small stove, I heated water for Chad's coffee and my hot chocolate. Those warm brews, along with slices of dry toast and strawberry jam, felt good in our stomachs. My fear was that we would knock over our hot drinks and they would leak through the cracks onto some poor hiker on the lower level. Thankfully, that disaster never happened.

That day, Spence Field Shelter resembled an international airport when all flights have been cancelled and passengers are waiting around in chairs and on floors for the next flight. We didn't have suitcases, but our backpacks were hanging from the shelter's rafters.

At one point, a new hiker came in from the rain and saw another image. He took one glance around the shelter and said, "This looks like a scene out of *Braveheart*." He was referring to the opening scene of that film, when the hero, a boy at the time, enters a barn and discovers dozens of Irish patriots hanging by their necks from overhead beams. I had to admit that the hiker's observation was pretty accurate. Those suspended backpacks did look like hanging bodies.

The dismal weather and crowded conditions put my emotions in the tank. I was reminded that hiking the AT produces a lot of emotional ups and downs. One hour I would be filled with enthusiasm for reaching Maine, and the next hour I was ready to pack it in and leave the trail. At that moment, I wasn't even sure I could reach the next shelter.

There, on the upper perch of Spence Field, I desperately felt the need to strengthen my soul. I dug out my New Testament and read a chapter. Just meditating on God's Word was a great help in restoring my soul and renewing my courage. I didn't have to be dominated by miserable weather and discouragement: God's presence was sufficient.

Feeling better, I could now observe what was happening around me. Hikers from different backgrounds and walks of life all were conversing about the latest weather report. The cold was taking its toll. Someone yelled, "Anyone have an extra sweatshirt?" and someone else came up with a sweatshirt. There is, I observed, cordiality in the miserable conditions.

One unusual feature of the group was five British soldiers, all young and in good shape, who yesterday had easily passed us on the trail as they jogged by in military shorts. They were now complaining of the cold.

"We were told to prepare for hot weather," said one of the soldiers.

A woman near them, surprised by that remark, said, "We were told to prepare for any weather."

The woman had expressed my sentiments, and I began to wonder about the British stiff upper lip.

At 11:00 that morning, the rain stopped, and Chad and I, along with others, decided to take a chance and resume hiking. Our packs weighed a ton because we now carried a wet tent and a wet towel that had been left outside. I tried to wring the water out of the towel but did a poor job because my hands were so numb with cold.

The rain returned later as we struggled up and over Thunderhead Mountain. The wind blew so fiercely that we struggled just to stay on our feet. At one point, we stopped and took refuge under a tree. With rain from the tree branches dripping on us and the cold penetrating us, I took out my little propane stove and heated up some chicken soup, just to keep us going. We huddled around the little flame for some warmth. It was a miserable scene, and blowing on our steaming cups of soup, Chad and I felt more like homeless tramps than proud Appalachian Trail hikers. Our courage was close to taking another nosedive.

"Always the Hard Way, Sir" (West Point Motto)

After six miles of hiking, we reached Derrick Knob Shelter. I suggested we pack it in and spend the night at the shelter, but that resulted in a minor dispute because Chad wanted to press on. Fortunately, he gave in when he saw that most of our fellow hikers were calling it a day. With the temperature in the forties, the strong wind and rain were just too much for everyone to continue. Conditions like that make hypothermia a real threat. Thankfully, a fire was blazing in the shelter.

The next morning, many of the hikers, including the British soldiers, announced that they were turning back because they couldn't take the weather conditions. I told Chad that the weather was so miserable that I almost was sorry I'd invited him to join me on this section. He didn't complain, and I was proud of the way he was handling the adversities. His sturdy enthusiasm and optimistic spirit made him a great hiking partner.

The lessons we were learning in the rain and mud were not without meaning, and they were as beautiful in their own way as flowers and sunsets. Deep down, we wanted trials like this. It was one of the reasons we were on the AT. A wise man once said, "Who really wants it easy, anyway?" In getting away from soft civilization and pushing ourselves, we were discovering our potential and drawing on God's strength in new ways. We were, as my jogger poster said, venturing beyond our limits.

At the next shelter, which was as crowded as the others, we met a friendly couple in their late fifties. The husband, a retired military man, had taken the trail name of Forward March. His wife was Swamp Yankee (what the people from her hometown of Cincinnati were called). Before zipping up his sleeping bag for the night, Forward March announced to his wife that they would be getting up at 3:00 A.M. to hike to Hump Mountain to watch the sunrise, which was supposed to be fantastic.

At 3:00, right on cue, I heard Forward March wake up Swamp Yankee for the hike to Hump Mountain and the sunrise.

"I'm not going," she replied in a grouchy voice and went back to sleep.

In my sleeping bag, I chuckled to myself and wondered how Forward March, the military man, felt about having his commands disobeyed.

The next day we reached Clingman's Dome, the second highest mountain in the eastern United States. I thought we would see some inspiring views, but it was not to be. The area was thick with fog, and visibility was zero. We climbed to the observation tower but couldn't see a thing. The place was swarming with disappointed adolescents, who looked at us as though we were aliens from outer space. And after five days in the wilderness, that's probably what we looked like.

It was only eight miles from Clingman's Dome to Chad's car at Newfound Gap. We already had decided to spend the night at Gatlinburg, Tennessee, and the prospect of a hot shower and a good meal quickened our steps. We arrived at Newfound Gap at 3:00 in the afternoon. We threw our damp, dirty packs in the trunk and headed for Gatlinburg.

This was our first visit to this tourist mecca, and we were unprepared for the shock. Coming out of quiet forests into crowded streets filled with cars and honking horns overwhelmed us. We felt like Tarzan in New York City and were momentarily disoriented and frustrated.

Eventually we overcame our emotions and found a motel. After showers, shaves, and changes of clothes, we felt much better and headed for a restaurant. Applebee's® was nearby and proved to be a good choice. The waiter seated us at a table on a large outdoor patio next to a rushing mountain stream. Perfect! We had the best of both worlds. We downed glasses of Sprite®, one after the other, and ate our meal of roast chicken with all the trimmings.

After dinner we leaned back and glowed with contentment and thanksgiving, savoring the delightful rest that only weary bodies can enjoy. Beside the mountain stream, we talked of our experiences and how we felt about them. Both Chad and I agreed that we had matured and grown in our relationship, which to me was the greatest blessing.

Temptation's Torment

The next morning, May 17, Chad returned me to Newfound Gap, as planned. From there, my son would head for Indiana, while I continued on the trail, hiking alone for the first time.

I was struggling. Part of me wanted to press on to new adventures on the trail, and another part pleaded to stay in Chad's car and return to our cozy home in Ohio. There I would have a hot shower every day—two, if I wanted—and all the goodies my heart could desire. No more rain and cold. My loving wife would rub my shoulders with delightful-smelling Hot Ice. I would sleep in our queen-sized bed with its unbelievably soft pillow-top mattress. And I would not have to endure this cruel separation from my family. Chad and I could spend another day together in the car on the drive home. I said nothing to Chad, but these temptations tormented my soul during the drive back to the AT.

In the end, courage and faith won out, and "Braveheart" (thinking of the movie again) would continue hiking. We got out of the car, and after a word of prayer and a final hug, I hoisted my pack to my shoulders and started off down the trail. When I had walked about fifty yards, I turned and looked back. Chad was still standing by the car, his gaze following me, as though the separation was hard for him too. He gave a final wave, and I waved back.

The path turned a corner, and I entered the woods, where I was no longer visible. I heard the car start, the gears shift, and the horn blow twice as the green Jeep headed north. I was alone for the first time on the Appalachian Trail. How would I handle it?

Chapter 7

Hot Springs Hotbed

For what shall it profit a man if he gains the whole world
and loses his own soul?

—Mark 8:36

New Found Gap to Erwin, Tennessee

In 1948, Earl Shaffer, still recovering from his World War II experiences, made history by becoming the first person to solo-hike the entire Appalachian Trail. He referred to his journey as "The Lone Expedition." That title expressed my feelings now as I hiked the AT for the first time without a companion. I was alone and feeling lonely on day six of my third section hike, but the Lord hadn't forgotten me.

After my son's departure, a cheerful morning sun came out, and twenty minutes later, I came upon a wooden sign pointing to a blue-blazed side trail. The sign said that the side trail, with the unusual name of "Boulevard," climbed five miles to the summit of Mount LeConte. Reading that name brought back warm memories. Nineteen years before, the summer of 1977, my wife and I had climbed Mount LeConte with our three sons, aged ten, eight, and five. On our third furlough from France, we decided that a climb and an overnight stay on Mount LeConte would be a great family vacation.

After a vigorous hike to the top of LeConte, we lodged in one of several rustic cabins. A more than ample supper in the dining hall was followed by a short walk with other hikers to admire a beautiful sunset. The most memorable part of that activity was that while we were ogling the sunset, a bear broke into one of the cabins, seized a woman's backpack, tore it open, and scattered her underwear all over the woods. Our family still laughs at that experience.

Standing again at the foot of Mount LeConte, nineteen years later, I spent a few moments praising God for my family and the wonderful memory of that climb. My heart encouraged, I continued on my way.

A short time later, I came to Icewater Shelter, where Forward March and his wife, Swamp Yankee, were eating breakfast. I greeted them and learned some bad news: Swamp Yankee would have to leave the AT because she was having serious problems with her foot and hiking had become too painful.

Knowing what a tough decision this was for them, I expressed my regrets and tried to encourage them. I gave them a gospel tract as well. Offering a tract seemed like a feeble gesture, but God uses the weak things of this world to accomplish His purposes.

The next fifty miles were good hiking and good weather. In fact, the weather was too good, because the sun was getting to me. Unfortunately, I had not brought sunscreen. Although most of the AT is shaded by trees, here and there are open stretches. I just had hiked a whole day through such a section, and my face and arms were burning.

MOUNTAIN MOMA REST STOP

Soon I came across handmade signs advertising a store off the trail called "Mountain Moma's," and I thought that perhaps I could get something there for my sunburn. An added attraction was the huge cheeseburgers the signs advertised.

I made good time to the downhill turnoff trail, and then I walked the two miles from the AT to Moma's on a road walk. Having been again exposed to the sun, I arrived hot and sweaty in early afternoon. Food and a shower would be more than welcome.

Hot Springs Hotbed

Mountain Moma's Kuntry Store, in North Carolina, was a study in backwoods southern culture. Parked in front of the store was a truck trailer with a sign that read: "Trust Jesus, not religion." I certainly agreed with that. Next to the truck was another sign, advertising different brands of cigarettes. Even though I remembered that tobacco grew in the south and smoking was big, I did not agree with that.

Curious as to what I would find, I took off my pack and entered the store. I noticed immediately that the walls were covered with memorabilia from the early 1900s. There were slogans encouraging people to drink Coke and use brands of soap and other items that no longer existed. A large picture of Dolly Parton hung on the wall. Large, plastic, white tracks on the wood floor led to the restroom. In the corner was a piano that looked like it belonged in a saloon, and in another corner, there was a flashing red neon sign declaring: "Jesus is Lord." It was a Cracker Barrel®, but a lot more authentic.

I asked a waitress about "Moma" and was told that she was in Dollywood® that day. That figured. A man in his fifties, whom I assumed was the owner, approached me. My trail book said his name was John, so I asked, "Are you John?"

"What's left of him," he replied.

As we talked, I noticed that he treated me with the usual suspicion that southerners reserved for northerners. But as soon I mentioned that I knew Charlie Watts, John opened up and talked more freely.

I asked him how long he had been a Christian, and he said, "Not near long enough." I gathered that he had been saved later in life and regretted not finding the Lord when he was younger.

I took a booth and ordered one of the famous cheeseburgers. When it arrived, the waitress placed it on the table. "Thar," she said.

I chuckled at her accent and ate the huge burger slowly, savoring each bite. While eating, I looked at a small TV set across the room, which was showing what appeared to be an all-day gospel sing. A tenor soloist dressed in a pastel pink blazer sang, "Little is much when God is in it." I was touched by the words and thought of my hike and what a small, humble mission it was. Yet because God was in it, my journey would have eternal significance.

I finished my burger and took a stroll around the area. In the back were several cabins for hikers, and beyond them was a swift mountain stream. As soon as I saw the stream, I knew what I wanted to do. I retreated to a restroom, changed into jogging shorts, then slipped into the stream's frigid waters. The icy water flowing over my hot, sunburned body was absolutely delightful. I relaxed in the water until numbness from the cold forced me out. That cold dip was just what I needed.

The swim was followed by a shower. One of the staff had given me a large bath towel, and as I walked to the bathhouse, I put it to my nose and inhaled. The smell of that cotton towel almost intoxicated me as I breathed in its clean, sweet fragrance. My wilderness experience was giving me a new appreciation for the simple things of life.

Several other hikers, including a young woman in her early twenties named Lilac, had landed at Mountain Moma's the same day. I first had met Lilac in a shelter several nights before. She had fallen sick and kept us shelter mates awake with her coughing and frequent visits to the woods. Now she was at Moma's, trying to recuperate from whatever bug she had picked up.

In talking with Lilac, I learned that she was Canadian and had attended a concert at the Christian college in Alberta that I had attended forty years before. This coincidence might seem strange, but actually it was not all that unusual. I kept bumping into people on the trail who were in some way connected to people and places I knew. The expression "It's a small world" was continually being confirmed to me.

I was even more surprised when Lilac told me she was a correctional officer in a prison in British Columbia; she seemed too petite and timid for that job. During our conversation, I talked to Lilac about God's plan of salvation. She listened as I read from the book of Hebrews, emphasizing the question: "How shall we escape if we neglect so great a salvation?"

Lilac said she was a member of the United Church of Canada but was confused about spiritual matters. I gave her my testimony and urged her to accept Christ as her Savior. Lilac's hesitant response indicated to me she was not ready to take that step. I asked if I could pray for her, and she agreed. I asked God to watch over her and help her to put her trust in Him.

The next morning, after a good night's sleep at Mountain Moma's cabins, I felt rested and ready to roll. The trail town of Hot Springs, North Carolina, about twenty-three miles to the north, was my next destination. According to the hiker manuals, Hot Springs was historic, so I was looking forward to visiting it.

One addiction of hiking the AT is the many discoveries the hiker makes. Every day he goes into virgin territory, exploring places he has never seen before. This phenomenon motivates the AT hiker to push onward. I guessed it was the same spirit that drove the pioneers westward in the early days in America.

Later that day, I reached Max Patch Mountain. The view from the top of Max Patch was magnificent—beauty stretched as far as the eye could see. Other hikers, awed by the same view, were sprawled on the grass. I was tempted to do the same, but the sun was hot, and even with the sun screen I'd bought at Mountain Moma's, I didn't want to risk too much exposure.

JONAH IN NINEVEH

The next day, May 23, I hiked an enjoyable fourteen miles and arrived in the famous trail town of Hot Springs. As always, one of my first concerns was lodging; so I stopped at the Jesuit Hostel on the edge of town but found it closed, with no reason given. I moved on to another hostel and learned that it was full.

Pack on my back, I walked down the tree-lined main street of Hot Springs. I knew of one other hostel, the Inn at Hot Springs. Having read about the place, I suspected it was a hotbed of the New Age movement—yet I had the uncomfortable feeling that the Lord wanted me to stay there that night. Although I did not relish an encounter with New Agers, like Jonah dragging his feet to Nineveh, I turned my steps toward the inn.

I approached the large, white Victorian house and saw a sign that said simply, "The Inn," and a smaller sign directing hikers to the back door. I went around the house and found a long back porch cluttered with the backpacks and hiking gear one would expect at a hiker hostel.

A couple in their forties was just emerging from the back door. The large woman, obviously not a hiker, wore a white t-shirt with "Denial" printed on it.

Someone on the porch asked her the meaning of her t-shirt, and she replied, "I deny everything."

She certainly is in the right place, I thought. And as the woman continued talking, I gathered that she and her male friend came to the inn often to immerse themselves in New Age teaching and the atmosphere that went along with it.

I pushed open the screen door, walked in, and found myself in a spacious kitchen. A man around thirty was at the stove preparing food that had all the aroma of a vegetarian meal. The man seemed to eye me suspiciously, or was it just my imagination? As a Christian in this den of New Age lions, I felt like a marked man.

Elmer, the director, wasn't around, so I asked the cook if there were any rooms left, hoping he would say they were filled up. But he replied that they had one room left. I glumly concluded that this must be where the Lord wanted me to stay. I went to the room and leaned my backpack against the one remaining bed. Jonah had arrived in Nineveh.

While I waited for a shower to become available, I looked around downstairs and entered a reading room off to the left. The décor was dark and heavy, turn of the century. One end of the room contained several musical instruments that appeared to be oriental. In the music corner were three sturdy wooden chairs with kneeling pads that looked like they belonged in a Catholic church.

Although I couldn't put my finger on it, something sinister pervaded the room. Maybe my imagination was working overtime, but I thought of Frank Perretti's book *This Present Darkness* and felt plunged into the atmosphere of that book.

Many of the volumes that lined the shelves promoted Chinese mysticism and far-eastern religion. Everything in the room seemed geared to leading young hikers away from God's truth and toward false religion. The place was the New Age version of Frances Schaeffer's *L'Abri* in Switzerland. No wonder I felt uncomfortable; it was the reaction of the Spirit of God, who dwells within me.

After my shower, I changed clothes and stretched out on the bed. Alone in the room, I prayed, claiming divine protection through Christ's blood. I remembered that God had not given me a spirit of fear, but of power and love and a sound mind (2 Tim. 1:7). I felt peace again as I walked downstairs.

At supper that evening, a dozen of us, mostly hikers, gathered around the table. When the platters of vegetarian food were served, I had a decision to make. Should I bow my head and thank God for my meal, as is my custom, or pray silently with eyes open to avoid any censure by the others? For me, there was no question. I would not be ashamed of the gospel of Christ. There in the bastion of occultism, I bowed my head and thanked God for the food and for the privilege of openly identifying with the One who had suffered on the cross for my sins.

Elmer, the congenial director, sat at the head of the table, presiding over all that took place. As the meal progressed, he directed the conversation, which was actually more of a monologue laced with New Age thinking. Although it was all very low-key, I wondered how many thousands of times Elmer had done this and into how many young minds he had sown the seeds of humanism. No doubt he had the best of intentions, sincerely thinking he was leading them into a richer life; but what he was giving them was cyanide for the soul.

What a tremendous thing it would be, I thought, *if there were Christian hostels along the Appalachian Trail, where young hikers could stay and be immersed in a biblical worldview*. I prayed that this might happen, that churches and Christian organizations might get a vision for such a ministry that would reach thousands of young hikers, many of whom are looking for answers and a reason for living.

The next morning after breakfast at the inn, I found the hiker register. I picked it up and stepped out to the front porch to write my thoughts. Seated in a wicker chair, I opened the book and began to write, but I was stuck. I wanted to leave a testimony for Christ for those who followed me, but I could think of nothing both forceful and appropriate.

The only words that came to me were the words from an old gospel song: "This world is not my home. I'm just a passin' through." *That doesn't sound very forceful*, I thought, but as I wrote the words in the book, I realized that simple sentence encapsulated the chasm that eternally separated Christianity from the humanistic philosophy promoted at the inn. The people at the inn were living for this present world, but Christians arc living for the glorious world to come, when Christ will reign as King of kings. Sitting on the porch of the inn, I was much comforted by that simple insight.

Francis Asbury: Evangelist on Horseback

Departing the inn, I walked down the main street and passed a church courtyard with a marble marker dedicated to the memory of the famous Methodist preacher Frances Asbury. Two hundred years before, Asbury had traveled 100,000 miles on horseback through these same North Carolina mountains preaching the gospel. In spite of roaming robbers, hostile tribes, rain and snow, and severe chronic bronchitis, he persevered in his mission of sharing the good news with lost sinners. Over the years, thousands of people became converted through his preaching.

Could something of the same passion that drove Frances Asbury be present in my small endeavor? My witness seemed insignificant next to the ministry of that great man of God. However, I knew that the same Spirit of Christ who dwelt in Asbury lived in me. Were we not, after all, kindred spirits and fellow missionaries?

I headed north singing, "Lead on, O King Eternal." This was my song as I walked toward new adventures with Christ on the Appalachian Trail.

The Appalachian Trail

1997
277.3 miles hiked

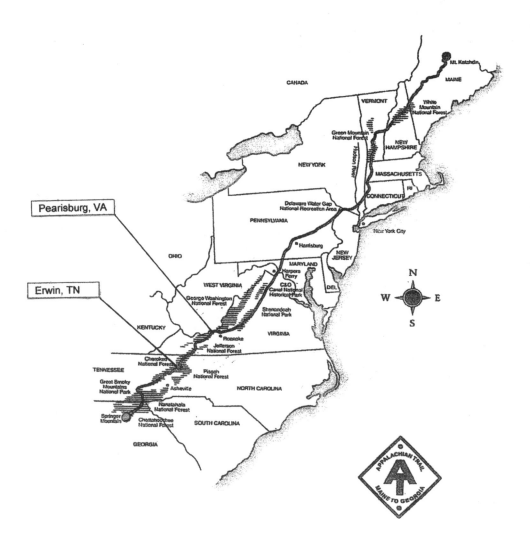

Chapter 8

Patriot Soldiers Marched Through Here!

O Lord, our Lord, how excellent is your name in all the earth.

—Psalm 8:9

Erwin, Tennessee, to Dennis Cove Road

My 1996 eighteen-day hike had ended on May 29 at Erwin, Tennessee, with a phone call to my wife in Ohio. We had been living temporarily with her parents while we looked for a home of our own. During my absence, Babs had found a house that seemed to be what we were looking for. It had a beautiful kitchen, air conditioning, a wood-burning fireplace, and a woodsy backyard. And, it was reasonably priced. It sounded perfect, but I had to return to Warren to seal the deal. I caught a Greyhound bus out of Erwin and traveled all night to reach Akron the next day. There my wife picked me up at the bus station. That evening, we visited the house and decided on the spot to buy it. Our weeks of frustrating house hunting were over.

It was now May 19, 1997, and I was back on the AT. Chad once again was my hiking partner. We had left his Jeep at Elk Park, North Carolina, and been shuttled back to Erwin, where we began hiking north on the next section.

On May 21, we climbed Roan Mountain (also known as "Groan Mountain") and were exhausted by the time we reached the top. Dead tired, we arrived gratefully at Roan High Mountain Shelter, an interesting two-story structure that once had been a fire tower. It was reputed to be the oldest shelter on the AT.

The old fire tower had an upper level that promised to be less humid than the ground floor. However, to get to the second floor, one had to crawl up a wooden ladder to an opening that was just big enough for a hiker without his pack. Our heavy packs had to be pulled and pushed through the opening. After some effort, both we and our packs reached the upper loft.

We had just gotten settled when a head popped through the opening. "Hey, I know you," the head's owner said.

Sure enough, it was Harry, a thirty-something-year-old hiker I had met on the trail the year before. We had been together only briefly the previous year, but on the trail, friendships are made quickly.

Harry seemed genuinely glad to see me. He climbed into the loft and began talking. He confided that he had abandoned his thru-hike the previous year and returned home because of an alcohol addiction. Shortly after leaving the trail, his brother's sudden death brought a big change in Harry's life. He quit drinking, joined Alcoholics Anonymous, and now believed in a higher power. Harry had returned to the AT determined to finish his thru-hike all the way to Maine.

I told Harry I was really happy for the new direction in his life and the steps he had taken. But I said that believing in a higher power falls far short of having a personal relationship with a loving God through faith in Christ. The year before, Harry had not been open to spiritual things, but now he listened carefully to what I said and seemed touched by it. He accepted the gospel tract I offered him, and he promised to read it. I was convinced that the crossing of our paths again had not been an accident. The "Hound of Heaven" was on Harry's trail.

The temperature dropped to below freezing that night on Roan Mountain. During the night, I awakened shivering and promised myself that I would invest in a down-filled sleeping bag as soon as our finances permitted it.

Chad and I hiked only six miles the next day. We were still tired from the climb up Roan Mountain; besides, the mountains, covered with wild flowers, were enchanting. We decided to take our time and "smell the flowers" because we probably never would pass that way again.

At Yellow Mountain Gap, we crossed Bright's Trace, famous because in the winter of 1780, one thousand patriot soldiers marched north through the gap on their way to defeat the British army. The patriot soldiers marched 170 miles, some of it through snow. I was moved as I thought of the brave men who had walked over the same ground on which we were treading. In my heart I saluted those tired, ragged soldiers and thanked God for an America conceived in liberty.

Shortly after passing Bright's Trace, we reached the Overmountain Shelter. As soon as I saw it in the distance, I knew I wanted to spend the night there. Overmountain Shelter was unusual; it was a large, red barn from which the lower half of one side had been removed to make a shelter for a dozen hikers. The enclosed loft upstairs would hold another dozen. Overmountain Shelter looked over the lovely valley spread out before us.

Chad and I staked our claim of a spot on the ground floor and then laid out our sleeping bags on the grassy slope in front of the shelter and took a delightful half-hour nap. Basking in the sun, I felt so content that I wrote in my journal, "Today I feel like a king."

Later we prepared and ate a leisurely supper, all the while admiring the pastoral panorama. It was backpacking at its most enjoyable: peaceful surroundings, pleasant fatigue, satisfied stomachs, and the freshness of the outdoors. It just didn't get any better than that.

By 8:30 we were ready for bed. The night promised to be cold again, so I wore my red wool ski hat and a sweatshirt to bed. After exchanging good-nights, we burrowed deep into our sleeping bags and were soon in dreamland.

Two hours later, I awakened and was startled to discover the silvery brightness of a perfectly-full moon flooding our sleeping area and the valley beyond. The moon seemed so close that I could reach out and touch it. I was so enraptured that I woke Chad so he could enjoy that spectacular moment with me. He opened one eye, mumbled, "Awesome," and fell back to sleep.

So much for sharing a spectacular moment, I thought.

Unlike Chad, I was in such awe that I lay awake for a long moment, bathing in the brilliance of the moonlight and praising God for His power and the priceless privilege that was mine to be on the Appalachian Trail.

The next morning, we left Overmountain Shelter. I knew that the memory of that place never would leave me. I always would remember and treasure the exquisite experience God had given me there, along with the dozens of other unforgettable experiences I was having on the AT—not the least of which were my five days with Chad, which had been rewarding. We had built some more good memories during our time on the trail together.

Chad and I set out for Elk Park, North Carolina, our destination for the next day. There we would meet my two younger sons, David and Mark. Unfortunately, Chad would have to return to his work in Indiana, but we would have the evening and next morning together. Living in different parts of the country, it was not often that the four of us got together.

David and Mark arrived the next day and joined Chad and me in our motel room in Elk Park. I was very happy to have my three sons with me, if only for a short time. We went out to a restaurant, and though the conversation was strained at times, we enjoyed the evening. Sibling rivalries die a slow death, and I had noticed that rapport was always harder when the four of us were together. One-on-one was always easier.

After a big breakfast at a restaurant the next morning, we squeezed into Chad's Jeep and drove to the trailhead. There we took photos and prayed, and then Chad left for Indiana. The remaining three of us— David, Mark, and I—began hiking.

For once, the first miles of our hike were not accompanied by rain. In fact, we had lovely weather while hiking through stands of pine trees and pastoral settings the first day. One would expect my mood to be upbeat, especially while hiking with my sons, but that was not the case. For some reason I again was assailed by negative thoughts, and the temptation to abandon my hike was strong. For a few hours I actually hated the AT and was despondent; although, I hid my struggles from my sons.

I suspected that eventually my mood would change, and I was right. Later that day I recovered my positive outlook. I was learning, painfully, that the greatest challenge in hiking the AT is not a physical one, but rather a battle with attitude. I'm convinced that the majority of hikers who abandon their dream of reaching Katahdin do so not because of physical problems but because of frayed and negative emotions. Come to think of it, that's why a lot of people drop out of life too.

David, our middle son, was the brain of the family (his math teacher in France had described him as "brilliant"). This was his first hike on the AT. David was married and the father of two girls. His family and a highly-successful career as a computer software engineer didn't leave him much free time, but he had managed to get away for a few days.

While growing up, David always had been something of a free spirit—always running ahead of us on family hikes. At age twenty-eight, he hadn't changed. Conventional wisdom says you hike up mountains slowly, especially at the beginning of a hike, but that advice was not for my son. He ran up the mountains and waited for us at the top, smug in his vigorous physical condition.

But late in the afternoon of the second day, his self-confidence caught up with him. At the top of one summit, we found David sitting on the ground, groaning in pain. He had been hit with severe leg cramps and couldn't walk another step. I resisted my see-I-told-you-so remarks and looked for a place to camp for the night. The options were not encouraging, but finally I found an area off the trail flat enough to put up our tents. I chuckled to myself as I carried David's pack to our camping spot while my athletic son hobbled along behind me. The Lord was teaching us all some valuable lessons on this hike.

The next morning, May 25, David's leg cramps were gone. We folded our tents and continued our hike. We had good weather that morning, but heavy rains returned in the afternoon. We donned ponchos and plodded on, and by late afternoon, we were thoroughly wet. In addition, Mark was weakened from a sudden bout of diarrhea, which is bad news when it's raining. (Trust me, keeping toilet paper dry in the woods when it's raining is a lost cause!)

We reached Dennis Cove Road cold, wet, and discouraged. We were about to cross over to the other side when David spotted a sign advertising a hostel and hot tub only a half-mile up the road. David was all for going there, but I resisted the idea. Were we wimps who caved in because of a little rain? Tempers rose as we argued over the issue, but thankfully, the Lord reminded me that we weren't hiking to prove how macho we were, but to have a good time together.

The hot tub won, and we were soon at Laural Fork Lodge, settled into a rustic cabin that greeted us with the pungent fragrance of freshly cut lumber. Supper was served, and a dozen cold, hungry hikers enjoyed a delicious meal as a heavy rain beat a drum rhythm on the metal roof above us.

With supper over, we put on shorts and headed for the hot tub, where our tired muscles rejoiced as we luxuriated in the hot water and steam. After spending a delightful twenty minutes joking and talking together, I had to admit that this wasn't a bad father-sons experience.

Back at the cabin, my sons were in the bunks next to mine—David on top and Mark on the bottom. I had a paperback copy of John Bunyan's biography and offered to read a chapter aloud before we fell asleep. My sons consented.

It was just like old times, when many years ago, I read to three little boys, bathed and in their pajamas, at bedtime. The little boys were now men, and I was proud and happy that they were my sons. We had our disagreements, even arguments at times, but we were growing in our relationships, and good relationships are the heart of family happiness.

By the time I finished reading the chapter, Mark had succumbed to sleep, weakened by his numerous trips to the woods that day, but David was still awake and listening. I ended our day with a prayer and turned out the lights. There had been some bumps in the road the last few days, but the Lord had helped us over them.

Chapter 9

The Loneliness of the Long-distance Hiker

I sought the Lord and He heard me.

—Psalm 34:4

Dennis Cove Road to Pearisburg, Virginia

The next morning we enjoyed the breakfast that the Lodge owners, Carl and Kate, had promised would "knock your socks off." I managed to keep my socks on while enjoying the delicious spread of homemade breakfast goodies: potatoes, fried eggs, biscuits with gravy—all the food hikers look forward to.

We then got a shuttle down Dennis Cove Road to a hostel called Braemar Castle in Hampton, North Carolina, where Mark had left his car. He and David would return to their homes in Harrisburg and Cincinnati, while I continued my trek north. We got to the car and, after the usual hugs, my sons drove off. At the time I had no idea how their departure would affect me.

Because Mark's car had been parked at Braemar Castle during our hike, I decided that it would be courteous to the owners for me to stay at Braemar that night. Besides, there was a sixty percent chance of rain that day.

That was a big mistake. No sooner had I settled in the hikers' quarters, in which I was the lone occupant, then I was hit by loneliness so severe that it felt like a blanket of darkness had dropped over me.

I realize now that several things were converging to contribute to this feeling: the weather was at its gloomiest, the hostel was old and discouraging, and weeks of hiking had depleted me physically. But most of all, I was knocked flat by the separation from my sons. I had always considered myself a strong person, but there I was, weeping and crying out to the Lord for deliverance from that slough of despair.

Finally, I was able to read some Scripture and sing several hymns I had memorized for just such an attack as this ("Be Still My Soul," "How Firm a Foundation," etc.). I read John Bunyan and felt like the weary Pilgrim making his way to the Celestial City. Like Pilgrim, I had many obstacles to overcome. My cloud of depression started to lift, and I felt some relief.

But then something else happened that day that turned my thoughts completely away from my emotional struggles. I was heating a can of chunky chicken soup for supper in the kitchen of the hostel when I heard a noise. Suddenly the door flew open, and in walked one of the most unusual hikers I was to meet on the trail. His appearance startled me. He was well over six feet tall and had a gray beard and long hair. Instead of the usual hiker attire, he wore faded Army fatigues, Army paratrooper boots, and a large leather belt with a buckle the size of a pancake. Attached to the belt was what looked like a huge bowie knife. How the man staggered up mountains with that heavy gear was beyond me.

The new arrival gave his trail name as Dead Man Walking, which did nothing to inspire my confidence in him. I began plying him with questions and learned that Dead Man Walking was 56 and that at age seventeen he had gone to South America to fight with the revolutionary Che Guevara. As he talked, I began to get the picture: the man was a throwback from the 1960s cultural revolution, a militant flower child grown old, so enamored with that period of history that he couldn't let go of it. He seemed to be living in the past, holding on to a cause that was relegated to the ash heap of history.

I tried to engage Dead Man in conversation, but it was not easy. His thoughts were not always coherent, and I wondered if drug use in the past was the reason. Still, I spoke to him of God's love and what Christ had done on the cross for us. But he appeared not the least bit interested in what I was saying.

My sleep that night was not exactly tranquil. Before I left the hostel the next morning, I gave Dead Man a tract with the title "Forgiven" and prayed that God would use it to open his heart and mind to God's simple plan of salvation.

Getting back on the trail lifted my spirits. Just moving toward the goal again helped me greatly in getting over the depression of the day before. Within an hour, I reached the side trail to Laural Falls and made the deep descent into the gorge where the falls are located. This famous cascade was as impressive as I had been told. I took photos, admired the beauty, and sang the "Doxology."

When I tried to leave Laural Falls, I couldn't find the trail blazes out of the gorge. Thinking they might be located on a ridge above the falls, I foolishly climbed up to the ridge to search for the blazes. Then I realized the precariousness of my situation. I was standing on slippery rocks on a very steep slope, and if I lost my footing, the weight of my heavy pack might very well plummet me down the slope, over an embankment, and into the falls. This was not a welcome prospect! So I stood there paralyzed, afraid to move.

Then, for some reason I looked at my watch. It was exactly 9:00 A.M., the time at which my wife and I had agreed to meet in prayer. The thought that she was praying for me at that very moment so encouraged me that I took heart, and by faith, I thanked the Lord for the way out of my predicament.

Taking care to move as little as possible, I eased my pack off and let it slide down the slope a couple of yards, where, fortunately, it caught on some rocks. I continued that process, carefully working my pack down the hill ahead of me. When I finally reached the bottom of the hill, I breathed a sigh of relief and thanked the Lord for my wife's prayers. I retraced my steps back out of the gorge to the AT. I was more convinced than ever that only by strong prayer support would I ever stand someday on the summit of Mount Katahdin.

Virginia, state number four on the AT route north, was just ahead. Of the fourteen states that the AT passes through, Virginia contains the longest section of trail.

DOWNTIME AT DAMASCUS

I was anticipating my visit to Damascus, which sits on the border between North Carolina and Virginia. Damascus is known as the AT's friendliest trail town. Indeed, as I walked into Damascus, I got the impression that the town was hiker-friendly. There was even a log hiker shelter on the road leading into the village; although, I chuckled when I noticed a small sign beside the shelter that read "No camping."

I headed for the main hostel in Damascus, provided graciously by the Methodist church and called simply "The Place." The Place was a large, white, two-storied building. Walking into the hostel's main room on the ground floor, I found the typical hiker environment: several hikers sitting around on stuffed furniture—worn out by thousands of hikers who had passed through over the years—playing cards, and swapping the latest trail news.

There was the traditional announcement board on which were posted the usual requests for rides to somewhere or other, plus grim warnings about deadly ticks and Lyme disease. I wondered how many would-be hikers had been scared off the trail before they even started by such cheerful information.

Far more upbeat was a poster picturing Bill Irwin, the first blind hiker to complete the AT. He was the author of *Blind Courage*, the story of his epic hike. On the back of Bill's t-shirt was printed the Bible verse, "For we walk by faith and not by sight" (2 Cor. 5:7). That was cool. I wasn't visually challenged like Bill, but I knew that I would reach Maine only by a walk of faith.

When I went upstairs and found an empty bunk in one of the large rooms used for sleeping, I noticed right away that, at age 63, I was in the minority. All the other hikers appeared to be in their teens or early twenties. The Place was definitely a hangout for young people.

Also evident was the dirt; the floor was caked with mud from hikers' boots, and a week's worth of dust and trash littered the room. A sign said that cleaning was on a voluntary basis, and it was obvious that volunteers were not standing in line to clean.

Deciding to set a good example, I found a broom and began to sweep the room where I and a dozen other hikers were lodging. As I swept, Rosebud, a blond hiker in her early twenties, walked into the room. Rosebud was unusually attractive, and unlike most female hikers on the AT, her hiking shorts were decidedly short, giving the impression that she was interested in more than just hiking. The young male hikers were not slow to pick up on this detail.

As Rosebud walked by me that day, I felt the Holy Spirit prompting me to talk to her about the Lord. Because we had exchanged greetings on the trail several times, I felt free to speak to her. I wasn't sure how to open the conversation, but I decided to take the plunge; so I stopped sweeping and leaned on the top of my broom. "Rosebud, do you ever think about the fact that God loves you and has a wonderful plan for your life?"

If I had hit Rosebud on the head with a baseball bat, her reaction could not have been more startled. Her head dropped, her eyes closed, and in almost a whisper she said, "I think about it every day."

Sensing that the Holy Spirit was speaking to this young woman, I outlined in a few words what she needed to do to get right with God. I knew I had only minutes to talk with Rosebud before another hiker would enter the room and disturb the privacy of that moment. But God can speak volumes in a few words, and I was confident that He was working in her heart. Behind Rosebud's brazen exterior was a soul struggling with the conviction of sin. Just then, another hiker walked in. I never saw Rosebud again after Damascus, but I continue to pray for her.

Before I left Damascus the next morning, I attended a small Baptist church of about forty people. The singing was slow and the message mediocre, but I'm convinced that this little group of believers, and the tens of thousands like it in our land, are America's greatest strength. As I hiked out of Damascus, I asked God to send a mighty revival to that little church and to all the churches in our land.

On the evening of June first, I reached the wilderness area near Mount Rogers and chanced on a lovely pond, which I immediately dubbed "Walden Pond." Pine trees grew around the edge of the pond, and their needles provided a soft bed for sleeping. I set up my tent, crawled in, and fell asleep serenaded by bullfrogs.

After a good night's rest, I rose early the next morning. As I prepared oatmeal for breakfast, I happened to look across the pond and saw a fawn coming down to the water's edge to drink. The serenity of that lovely scene gladdened my heart, as I understood that the same loving God who provided my breakfast was also meeting the needs of that little fawn. We were both the objects of His care. It was a touching picture that I have never forgotten.

A Night on Buzzard Rock

My surroundings the next night, however, were completely different. With much difficulty, I had climbed up Buzzard Rock, and now I was exhausted. The view from the summit of Buzzard Rock that evening of June 2 was inspiring, and I was tempted to spend the night there, but the wind was so strong that I knew it would be impossible to put up my tent.

I continued hiking another fifteen minutes and found on the other side of the mountain a site that was relatively sheltered from the wind. The only problem was that level ground is hard to find on the side of a mountain. I did my best to set up my tent anyway, knowing that I would not have a comfortable sleep that night.

The rain fell lightly, and the night was very dark. I lay on my stomach inside my tent, preparing my supper of sardines and a packaged pasta mix. I had placed my little propane gas stove in the little "vestibule" at the entrance of my tent. Lying on your stomach is not a comfortable position for cooking or for eating, but I was thankful for the tent's shelter and warmth.

As I expected, sleep did not come easily as I struggled to find a comfortable sleeping position and counter the pull of gravity. On that starless night in the barren wilderness, I felt strangely all alone, as if I were the only person on planet Earth. Was this, I wondered, how Moses felt in the backside of the desert?

People have wondered what a hiker thinks about when alone in the wilderness. I turned to comforting memories. I thought of a long-distance hike with my wife in the Pyrenees Mountains in southern France when we were a young married couple. We followed a narrow highway through the mountains that led to the Spanish border. The memory of that walk came back to me. I could smell the special crispness of the Pyrenees mountain air, and in my mind's eye, I savored their beauty.

The first day of our walk, my wife and I had stumbled on an unused campground outside the village of Laruns, France, and decided to stay there. It rained hard that night, and water entered our tent. The next morning, we sought refuge in a tiny shower stall just big enough for two people. Sitting on the floor of the stall, we made oatmeal and played chess. We laughed, prayed, and rejoiced together in the grace of life.

That night on the backside of Buzzard Rock, the memory of that day with my wife filled my heart and my little tent with joy. Good memories are powerful comforters.

Two days later, I reached Mount Rogers National Recreation Headquarters. AT hikers were allowed to camp overnight at the headquarters, and several tents already were set up on the grassy area outside the main building. I decided to stay there for the night. Because this was my last night on the trail, I didn't use my tent but slept under an overhanging arch in order to get an early start the next morning.

I learned that it was possible to order pizza by phone from Dominos. Amazed by this possibility, I found an outside phone and had started to order when a voice said, "Hey, we've got plenty."

The voice belonged to a hiker named Connecticut Kid, hiking with his wife. This young couple had two huge pizzas and said they would like to share them with me. I accepted their kindness and offered to pay for my three slices, but they wouldn't hear of it. I was touched, especially when I learned that Connecticut Kid's wife had injured her leg and they were forced to give up their dream of reaching Katahdin. They were leaving the trail the next day and returning home, yet their deep disappointment did not keep them from thinking of others and sharing their pizza. The amount of goodwill on the AT often amazed me.

The temperature dropped to freezing that night, but despite the cold, I was up and on my way the next morning before daybreak. I was in a hurry because today I was going to see my wife! She was coming with her parents in their RV to Atkins, Virginia, where we had agreed to meet at a restaurant on Route 11 near the AT. Only ten miles lay between me and the end of my sixth section hike.

My last day of hiking, June 6, 1997, was euphoric. The fragrances from spring blossoms made the trail dreamlike, and flame azaleas lined some areas of the path. A few days earlier, a woman at a hostel had said that azaleas flower at Pentecost and look like the flaming tongues of fire described in the second chapter of Acts. It was a welcome reminder that the Holy Spirit was with me on the trail.

I now had completed one-fourth of the AT, having hiked 530 miles since my start in 1992. I had become a believer; by God's grace, I would reach Maine! With a bounce in my step, I hiked the last mile to the restaurant on route 11 and the glad reunion with my wife.

The Appalachian Trail

1998
382.2 miles hiked

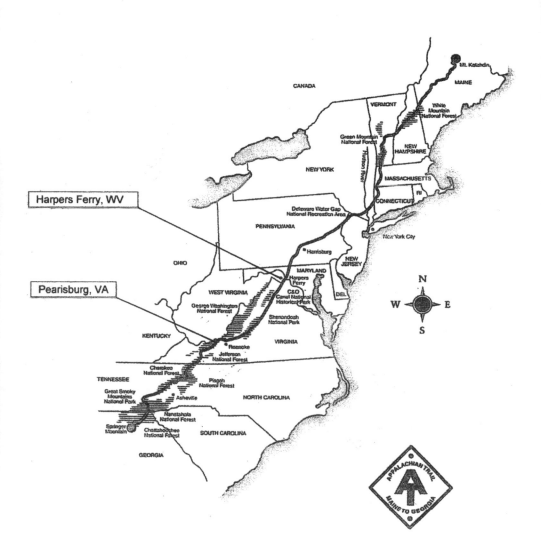

Chapter 10

Touched by
a Trail Angel

Oh, taste and see that the Lord is good.

—Psalm 34:8

Pearisburg to Catawba, Virginia

The spring of 1998 found me back in Virginia, ready to conquer new mountains and new trails. A Greyhound bus took me from Akron, Ohio, to Pearisburg, Virginia, the town I had reached in my hiking in the fall of '97. I was especially excited because my best friend and former missionary colleague, John Stauffacher, was scheduled to join me for the first week of my hike.

Always prompt, John arrived right on time at the hiker hostel in Pearisburg on May 4. He was one of those people you could count on in any situation. John was tall and thin and looked every inch the college professor he was. Having been born in Kenya of missionary parents, John spoke faultless French. He had a master's degree from Dallas Seminary and a doctorate in church history from the University of Strasburg in France. Yet, my dear friend's outstanding qualities were his humility and his servant heart.

After John changed into hiking clothes, we left for a point on the trail forty miles south of Pearisburg. We would pick up the AT there and return to Pearisburg from that point by hiking north. Bill, the manager of the Holy Family Hostel and my shuttle driver on several occasions, took us to the trail. Bill was a burly ex-Marine who delighted in recounting harrowing stories of hikers on the trail. His specialty was snake stories. He told with vivid detail the story of a hiker who died after being bitten on the bottom while taking care of a physical necessity in the woods. Between stories, Bill and I had good discussions on what it meant to be a Christian and to know for certain that our sins are forgiven and that we have eternal life. I appreciated his interest in spiritual matters.

We waved good-bye to Bill as he drove off. John and I started hiking on the AT under fair skies. I didn't plan to cover much ground that first day because I knew John was not in shape for long-distance hiking. But even the two-and-a-half miles to Helvey Mills Shelter had exhausted him, and when he saw the arrow pointing to the shelter, he gasped a relieved *"Merci, Seigneur"* (Thank you, Lord).

Adding to John's suffering was the fact that a well-meaning friend had loaded him down with backpacking equipment and more food than he needed. As a result, his pack was much heavier than it should have been. Although I tried to keep hiking mileage on the low side that week, I think John at times thought of our hike as something akin to the Bataan Death March.

On the positive side was the warm fellowship we enjoyed as we discussed spiritual matters and our experiences as missionaries in France. My friendship with John and his wife, Margaret, went back forty years to Bible College in Columbia, South Carolina, and we had fun remembering those nostalgic days.

On day four we came to the hiker haven I had been looking forward to—Woods Hole. John and I arrived there in a downpour, soaking wet. We changed into dry clothes, and then one of the workers led us to the rustic loft upstairs, where hikers slept on mattresses. There were only two sleeping spots left: one on a pile of four mattresses, and another, with only one mattress. Before I could open my mouth, John claimed the one-mattress bed, which was definitely less comfortable than the four-mattress bed. This was vintage John Stauffacher, always giving preference to another brother. I was touched—and rebuked—once again by John's humility and selfless life.

Breakfast the next morning was in silver-haired Tilly Wood's log cabin next to the hostel. Many years before, Tilly and her husband (now deceased) had turned their summer home into a refuge for weary hikers. Woods Hole was a monument to the generosity of those folks.

A cozy fire in one corner warmed the room as eight of us sat around Tilly's table which was loaded with eggs, sausage, grits, and biscuits. Before we ate, Tilly asked if one of us would give thanks to the Lord for the food. I volunteered, expressing my gratitude to God for this dear lady and the abundant food before us. Tilly was a congenial host, and the conversation was lighthearted and cheerful. For wayfaring hikers, this homelike atmosphere was a delightful treat.

After breakfast, John and I headed for Pearisburg with happy hearts and a quickened pace. The miles went by, and before we knew it, we were standing at Angel's Rest on Pearis Mountain, where we stopped to admire the spectacular view. It seemed only natural to read a few verses from the Bible and spend a moment in prayer. Our hike had not been easy, but the Lord had been good.

After a deep descent from Angels Rest, we made it to Pearisburg, where John and I said our good-byes. He would return to their furlough home in Florida, and I would continue hiking north. I could not have known that this would be our last hike together. My dear friend John died of cancer during the writing of this book. I always will treasure the memory of our week together on the Appalachian Trail.

The sadness I felt at John's departure was relieved by the arrival of my son Chad later that day. Chad definitely had Appalachian Trail fever and had begged off a week from his work as a purchasing agent for a steel company to hike the next section with me.

On May 14, my son and I had two big mountains to cross. It was tough going but rewarding; we crossed beautiful meadows with inspiring mountains in the distance and climbed over many stiles. Those wooden, ladder-like stiles could be annoying at times, but really, I was grateful for them—they beat tearing my pants on barbed wire! That day, Chad and I ate lunch in a lovely meadow covered with wildflowers and then lazed in the sun for a while. Oh, it was good to be alive!

By the end of the day, we had hiked a hefty fourteen miles and found ourselves on Sinking Creek Mountain with a breathtaking vista of the endless Blue Ridge Mountains. We dispensed with the tent that night and camped under the stars. Talk about "a room with a view"! When the stars and moon made their appearance, we were overwhelmed by their splendor.

Far below in Craig Creek Valley, lights of civilization flickered from homes that seemed a thousand miles from us. The full moon was so near that I pulled my billed cap down to shield my eyes from its brightness. And the stars—I could have reached out and plucked them. Chad and I fell asleep reveling in the awesome privilege of being on the Appalachian Trail and having front seats to this spectacular display of God's universe.

The temperature the next day was in the eighties. We came upon a spring with water more delicious than any I ever remembered tasting, so cold it made my teeth ache. A few minutes later, I was singing God's praises as we walked single-file on a narrow path. Chad, a few steps behind me, suddenly yelled out, "Papa, back away!" I jumped back just in time and saw on my left a large rattlesnake coiled and ready to strike. Chad had heard the rattle, I hadn't. I was thankful, yet I wondered what would happen after he and I parted, when I wouldn't have access to his keen hearing.

To our surprise, later that day we came on a memorial to Audie Murphy, the most decorated US soldier of World War II. A plaque several yards from the AT explained that on May 28, 1971, Murphy's private plane had crashed near where we were standing. He was forty-six years old.

Audie Murphy's life is a study in fame and tragedy. The son of poor Texas sharecroppers, he was celebrated for his courage as a soldier. Credited with killing 240 of the enemy in Europe and wounding and capturing many others, Murphy received every decoration for valor offered by a grateful America.

After the war, Audie Murphy was invited to Hollywood by actor James Cagney. He eventually made forty-four feature films and earned close to three million dollars. But the courageous Murphy had a weakness: he loved to gamble, and at the time of his death, he was heavily in debt.

Standing before Audie Murphy's memorial, Chad and I both felt the sadness of what might have been, and I couldn't help wishing that his life had ended happily. We shouldered our packs and moved on down the trail.

The next day, Chad and I climbed a fearful collection of rocks that were appropriately named "Dragon's Tooth." It was beautiful at the top but dangerous climbing down the other side, and I prayed that we wouldn't slip and break a leg. With the Lord's help, we made it safely to the bottom of Dragon's Tooth.

The rhododendrons were out in their spring glory, and lilies of the valley were in abundance. Their intoxicating fragrance never failed to lift my spirits. We were nearing Catawba, Virginia, where Chad would recover his car and end his hike with me for this year.

We were descending the hill that leads into Catawba when we spied a picnic cooler beside the trail. *What in the world?* A note taped to the cooler invited hikers to help themselves to cold drinks, sandwiches, and power bars inside the cooler. We couldn't believe our good fortune—we had heard of Trail Angels, but this was the first time we had been the recipients of their generosity.

It didn't take us long to open soda cans and start munching on sandwiches. We were enjoying our snack when we saw a bearded young man, the Trail Angel himself, walking up the hill towards us. With a smile, he introduced himself as Jeff Williams. Jeff explained that a few years before he had hiked half of the AT, and now, knowing what it was like to be hungry and thirsty on the trail, he just enjoyed providing refreshments for hikers.

We expressed our appreciation to Jeff for his thoughtfulness. As we talked, I felt led to ask him about his relationship with God. He said he had accepted Christ but had lingering questions for which I might have answers. We then had a profitable discussion, and I shared truth from the Bible about the eternal security of the believer. Our conversation with Jeff was even more refreshing than the snack from the cooler. With happy hearts, we walked the remaining distance to Catawba.

Chapter 11

Strange Dudes and Fear on the Skyline Drive

I will fear no evil; for you are with me.

—Psalm 23:4

Catawba, Virginia, to Bear Wallow Gap

Although Chad's third AT trek with me ended in Catawba, Virginia, I must recount a closing incident—a bad news/good news experience—in that adventure.

We were preparing to enjoy a good night of rest on soft beds at a motel not far from Catawba. While taking my shower, something was bothering me. I had the feeling that something was wrong. Then it hit me: the trekking poles. Where were the trekking poles?

I asked Chad if he had them, and he said "no."

After a brief discussion, we realized that the poles could only be in one place—leaning against the front of the store, where we had set them while we waited for our shuttle to pick us up that afternoon. In our haste to leave, we had forgotten the poles.

On the surface, the loss of hiking poles would not seem all that serious, especially to non-hikers. But to me, it was devastating. When I began my hike at Springer Mountain, I was certain that I did not need

75

hiking poles, thank you very much. Hiking poles were for old people. But a hundred miles and several painful falls changed my mind. While climbing Albert Mountain, I picked up a hiking stick that someone had tossed aside and found it helped me climb. I eventually bought some trekking poles that I found on sale in a backpacking store, and it was love at first use. I realized how helpful they were, not only in keeping my balance, but also in gaining traction as I climbed mountains. As one hiker expressed it: using hiking poles is like having four legs.

My poles were not ordinary—they were the hiker's Mercedes-Benz®. Made in the Czech Republic, they had double-spring action and cork handles, and they telescoped into one-third of their length. Even at sale price, they had cost almost a hundred dollars.

Losing my hiking poles was like losing my right leg. How could I hike without them? I had trouble sleeping that night, certain there was no way those poles would still be in front of the store the next day. The situation looked hopeless. With despair gnawing at me in the dark of that night, I asked the Lord to help us find the poles. The next morning, Chad and I left early for the convenience store, and when we pulled up in front of the store, my heart sank. The poles were nowhere in sight.

Perhaps the owner had noticed them the night before and kept them for us, we hoped. So we went into the store and explained our problem to the owner. We asked if he had seen them. To our dismay, he replied that he hadn't, and neither had his assistant. We walked out of the store, our faces clouded in disappointment.

We stood in front of the store pondering what to do. Then out of the blue, a thought struck me. I'm not often given to flashes of insight, but that morning, God gave me one. An almost audible voice said, "Look behind the store."

Looking behind the store sounded like a crazy idea, and I was sure we would find nothing, but I said to Chad anyway, "Let's check the back of the store."

We went around the corner of the building, and there on a small wooden porch were four beautiful trekking poles! My relief was so great that I shouted, "Praise the Lord!"

How had the poles gotten there? We could only surmise that some passing hiker had found the poles and put them where they would not be stolen. We will never know who that thoughtful person was, but we do know that God sent him or her at just the right moment because God takes loving care of His weak and forgetful children.

What a triumphant way to end our hike. Chad and I gave each other a final hug. Then he drove off with a loud honk, and I headed north on the trail with a light heart and the wonderful assurance that my heavenly Father was in control of this expedition.

My next challenge was the 2,000-foot climb to the top of McAfee Knob. The eighty-five-degree temperature only increased the difficulty. In several books about the AT, I had seen spectacular photos of hikers standing triumphantly on the summit of McAfee. I thought I might get someone to take a photo like that of me standing bravely on the edge of a precipice (if my acrophobia would allow me to get that close), only inches from a 2,000-foot drop. Such a photo would impress my friends, and maybe if I ever wrote a book, it could even be on the cover!

But that was not to be. When I got to the top of McAfee Knob, the haze was so bad that good photos were out of the question. My anticipated photo-op turned out to be a photo-flop. Disappointed, I walked around McAfee Knob imagining the beauty that I could see only dimly, and then I went on my way.

TINKER CLIFFS

Sooner or later, however, life's dark clouds give way to sunshine. I stayed at Campbell Shelter that night, and the next morning, May 17,1998, I headed for Tinker Cliffs, five miles away. After arriving at the Cliffs, I wrote in my journal:

> Glorious, glorious, glorious! I don't have words to describe my feelings and the beauty that I am beholding this morning. It's a gorgeous hiking day, and the view from Tinker Cliffs is out of this world—breathtaking; all that I ever hoped for on my AT hike.

I longed for Babs and my sons to be with me to enjoy all that I was seeing. Then I remembered that it was Sunday morning and at that moment people were gathering in grandiose churches. I would not have traded my glorious cathedral for the most expensive, stained-glass edifice in the world.

As I stood on the edge of Tinker Cliffs worshiping God and looking out on the vast panorama, with all the lung capacity I could muster and in my best tenor voice, I sang the great old hymn "How Great Thou Art." It just seemed so appropriate.

> O Lord my God, when I in awesome wonder
> Consider all the worlds Thy hands have made,
> I see the stars, I hear the rolling thunder, thy power
> Throughout the universe displayed
> Then sings my soul, my Savior God to Thee,
> How great Thou art, How great Thou art.*

I finished my twenty-minute worship service by singing all the stanzas of that hymn. Then, with a glad heart, I put on my pack and headed down the other side of Tinker Cliffs.

I had walked only a hundred yards when I met a teenage girl hiking toward the summit that I was leaving. The small backpack she carried told me she was a day hiker. As we passed each other on the trail, she smiled and we exchanged greetings. She continued on her way, and I then realized that someone else had attended my worship service that morning. In all probability, my voice had carried to that young girl as she drew near the summit and she had heard my song of praise to God. I wondered what the Holy Spirit had said to her as she listened to a lone hiker worshiping his Creator. One day I may know.

For the Appalachian Trail hiker, Virginia is the longest stretch (in terms of miles), of any state along the trail. That the Virginia AT seemed endless wasn't a problem for me because of all the beauty to see.

Strange Dudes and Fear
on the Skyline Drive

Virginia is definitely "the state for lovers"—especially lovers of God's creation.

In central Virginia, AT hikers become well acquainted with the famous Skyline Drive, also known as the Blue Ridge Parkway. For decades I had heard of this lovely ribbon of road that rolls through the Virginia Appalachian Mountains. And now, because the AT crosses the Blue Ridge Parkway dozens of times, I was getting to know that road firsthand.

The crossings never posed any problem for me because the traffic was usually light—so light, in fact, that the parkway struck me as being lonely. That impression no doubt had something to do with my reaction to a strange experience I had on that legendary road.

FEAR AT BEARWALLOW GAP

On Wednesday, May 20, the sun was setting as I reached Bearwallow Gap and mile 90.9 on the Skyline Drive. To rejoin the trail on the other side of the parkway, I had to follow the road about 150 yards. I walked slowly, glancing around for a tent site for the night. I saw one possibility, but because I felt it was too close to the road, I continued looking.

As I walked along the road, I became aware of an unusual stillness. There were no sounds whatsoever—no birds, no wind, no cars—just eerie, dead silence. I felt an uneasiness settle over me that I couldn't explain, knowing that I never had felt this way before on the trail.

A man's voice shattered the silence. At first I had no idea from which direction the voice was coming. Then, looking up at the small stone bridge I was about to pass under, I saw a man peering down at me. The young man had wild hair that came to his shoulders, but what startled me was the wild look in his eyes. At that moment my uneasiness turned to panic. I felt unnerved, but I made a great effort to conceal my fear.

"Any camping spots in these parts?" he asked in a rough voice.

As calmly as I could, I replied that I was looking for something myself. I immediately regretted that reply because it made me feel more vulnerable; I was admitting that I was homeless and alone.

Just then an older man stepped up next to Wild-hair, and I was relieved to see that he looked normal. He was wearing a blue plaid shirt and dark cotton pants, and behind him was a light-blue, battered pickup truck. We talked for a few minutes, the two of them standing on the bridge ten feet above me and I on the road. I wished desperately that a car would pass so that I wouldn't feel so alone, but none did. It was as though we three were the only people in Virginia.

Finally, after muttering about looking somewhere else, the two men got into their pickup and drove off. When they were out of sight, I breathed more easily and walked down the road another 50 yards to where the AT turned off to the right. I was disappointed to discover that from there the trail climbed Cove Mountain; there was no way I was going to put up a tent in that kind of terrain.

Fearing that I would be caught with no place to sleep when night fell, I remembered the camping spot I had rejected because it was too near the road. That would have to do for tonight, I decided. I had no other choice, so I walked the short distance back to the site. The ground was fairly level. I pulled out my tent and began setting it up.

I had just finished when I heard a noise. I turned around, and there was the same battered, light-blue pickup stopping on the side of the road. The two men got out of the truck, slammed the doors, and loudly argued about what they were going to do. Because my tent was so close to the road, I knew they had seen me. I felt trapped, and there was no place to hide.

I watched them from my tent site in the woods, only thirty yards away. Wild-hair picked up a foam mattress and a blanket and headed up the trail in my direction. For a second I feared he was going to camp next to me, but he continued up the trail without a word. The older man yelled to me from the road that he was spending the night in the pickup.

Great, I thought. *Now I'm sandwiched between these two guys.* It was not a reassuring situation.

I ate a bite for supper by flashlight and then crawled into my tent. Zipping up a tent door didn't give me any protection, but it made me feel safer. Then I remembered that my pack, which contained all my papers and money, was still outside. I reached into the darkness and pulled the pack into my tent.

I settled down for the night, but I couldn't sleep, and I couldn't stop thinking about those men. What were they doing here? They certainly weren't hikers, so who were they? Criminals fleeing from the law? Lying in my dark, fragile tent, all kinds of scary possibilities came to mind. I prayed for protection, asking God to help me in my weakness.

I woke the next morning before 6:00, dressed, and started to make breakfast. As I knelt in front of my gas stove, a voice from behind startled me. I stood and turned around to see the older man. He introduced himself as John and said that he hadn't slept well in the pickup. I didn't tell him that I hadn't sleep well either, or why.

John said that the long-haired man was his cousin, recently released from prison.

John was trying to help him. I was not surprised by the mention of prison. John said his cousin had visions, acted violently, and thought he was the Son of God.

I told him that his concern for his wayward cousin was commendable. Then I asked John about his relationship with the Lord. He said that he once had attended an evangelical church but had become angry with the pastor and left. When I tried to explain the gospel to John, he said he knew the Bible from cover to cover and didn't need any explanation. His answers to my questions were strange and confusing, and I soon suspected I was dealing with a man with some mental problems.

With our conversation going nowhere, I felt relief when the cousin came down the trail carrying his foam mattress and blanket and they announced that they were leaving. They climbed into their battered pickup and drove off with a roar and a cloud of dust. I was happy to see them leave.

I finished my breakfast, and then began one of my most painful moments on the trail. As I began packing my things, I realized that the zipper-lock bag containing my money, credit card, traveler's checks, and driver's license was missing. It was nowhere to be found. For twenty minutes, I searched desperately through my sleeping bag, backpack, and all of my clothes, not once but again and again. Nothing.

I cannot describe the feeling of desperation that swept over me. The vulnerability that had plagued me at times in the wilderness at this moment reached earthquake force. Never had I felt so completely helpless and afraid. With the loss of that zipper-lock bag, I had lost everything, including my identity.

In retrospect, I realize that the turmoil of my emotions was linked to my encounter with the two men, which had been traumatic. Thoughts that they might have stolen my valuables leaped to my mind. Could they have been con men? While I'd been talking to John, my back was to the tent and I was distracted. Had the cousin slipped in and stolen the zipper-lock bag while I wasn't looking? Thoughts like these—and others—tormented my mind.

There in my little tent, I was without answers and close to running out of hope. But that is the place where God meets us. I lay face down on the floor of my tent and cried out to the Lord. I finally told Him that if this was His way of doing a new work in my life, I would accept it. It was a hard prayer to pray, but it brought some comfort in knowing that the problem was in God's hands, not mine.

With a heavy heart, I put everything back into my pack and crawled out of my tent. Taking down the tent was always the last part of breaking camp. I took the fly sheet off the tent and began to fold it, and then I noticed something lying against the outside wall of my tent. I didn't have to look twice—it was my zipper-lock bag!

In an instant I understood what had happened. The night before, in dragging my pack into the tent in the dark, the zipper-lock bag had slipped from the open pocket of my pack and lodged between the outside wall of the tent and the fly.

By then I was an emotional mess, and all I could do was pour out my thanksgiving to God. Why He called me to go through this experience, I didn't know; but I did know He had some purpose for it.

I finished packing and started hiking up Cove Mountain, reflecting as I walked on what had happened. I concluded that, as with my bout of loneliness at the hostel, exhaustion had more than a little to do with my traumatic reaction to the two men and my supposed lost possessions. My physical and emotional resources were depleted from hiking hundreds of miles and climbing thousands of feet. My physical condition certainly needed to be considered. But there was something else, something deeper that had caused me to respond as I did. The Skyline Drive incident had uncovered a childhood fear that had been buried until that experience with the two men.

Strange Dudes and Fear
on the Skyline Drive

I was seven years old and walking downtown after school to see my mother, who worked in a drugstore. Weinberger Drug Store was only fifteen minutes away from Market Street Grade School, but it seemed longer than that to a seven-year-old. Halfway to the drugstore, I was accosted by three older boys. These ten-year-old hoodlums said that if I didn't give them a dime, they would beat me up. I was so afraid that I started crying. Fortunately, my crying drew the attention of some passersby, and the three boys fled.

When I reached the drugstore, I sobbed out my story to my mother, who, bless her heart, wiped my tears and gave me a mother's love. But the experience had left its mark on me. My parents divorced when I was a year old, and I grew up without a father. The threats from the three boys brought home to my young mind a grim reality: a fatherless boy has no protection. I was alone against the bullies of the world.

When I faced the threat of those men that day on the Blue Ridge Parkway, the little boy in me had reacted. I recognized that this was an area of my life that needed God's touch. It was not God's will that I live in fear. I needed to understand that when I accepted Christ as my Savior at age eleven, I ceased to be fatherless. I now had a heavenly Father who never would forsake me. He promised to be my shield and my strength in every situation. And though the Lord had tried to show me that truth many times over the years, this experience had brought the matter to a head.

As I climbed Cove Mountain, I asked the Lord to make me constantly aware of His presence and that I might put childhood fears behind me and walk confidently ahead in life with trust in Him. I wanted to remember Bearwallow Gap as a place of God's blessing.

Chapter 12

Harpers Ferry Fever

I will lead them in paths they have not known.
—Isaiah 42:16

Bearwallow Gap to Maupin Shelter

On May 21, 1998, I calculated that I was only 250 miles from Harpers Ferry, West Virginia, the philosophical (though not actual) halfway point on the Appalachian Trail. Halfway! Just pronouncing the words sent a shot of adrenalin through me. My heartbeat and my pace quickened as I set my sights on Harpers Ferry.

I hiked eleven miles that day, almost all of them uphill. But the day was so beautiful and my muscles were now so hardened that at the end of the day I felt good. At lunch I finished the pizza I had bought at a campground called JellyStone Park, and at around 5:00, I reached Thunderhill Shelter. Because the weather had turned cooler, it was easier to sleep, and I was sacked out by 8:00 P.M.

The next day, I met Grumpy and Speedy, who were thru-hiking together. Grumpy, about forty and of medium height, was a former US Navy Seal. Speedy, who was taller, was only nineteen and came from Germany.

Grumpy and Speedy were using the two-car system: they would leave a car at each end of the section they were hiking for the day, and then, one hiking north and the other south, they met at the section's midpoint and exchanged keys. Then at the end of the day, they would rendezvous at a predetermined campsite. It was not a system that I would have enjoyed, but it seemed to work for them.

Grumpy asked me if I would like to join them for supper at the end of that day. They would drive me to a nearby campground, and we could go out for supper together. It sounded good, so we decided to meet at a location just off the trail at 5:00.

I was on time for our meeting, and Grumpy and Speedy arrived a few minutes later. We went to Wildwood Campground, where I showered, shaved, and put on a clean shirt. (I always carried a clean shirt for just such occasions.) Then we left for the restaurant, and on the way, we squeezed two other hikers into Grumpy's car.

The two new hikers introduced themselves as Pilgrim and Jack. They were a young married couple from Florida, both in their late twenties. Jack was over six feet tall, and Pilgrim was only a few inches shorter than her husband. I detected right away that they were not in complete agreement as far as the thru-hike was concerned. Although hiking the Appalachian Trail had always been Pilgrim's dream, Jack was not a romanticist and did not hesitate to say that he was on the AT just to please his wife. His heart was not really in the adventure.

Grumpy's car pulled up to a restaurant that appeared to be the perfect sort of place for hikers. And it was; just reading the menu made my mouth water. I ordered the prime rib, which was served huge and juicy and accompanied by a baked potato dripping with butter. For dessert, I enjoyed a good-sized root beer float.

When the waitress brought our food, I offered to thank the Lord for our meal. Although the four appeared to be a little shocked, they agreed to my suggestion. In fact, all of my new friends seemed OK with the idea, except for Speedy, the German, who smirked when we bowed our heads. *Typical European reaction,* I thought.

The next morning, Grumpy and Speedy were already up and on their way when I awoke at 6:00. Wanting to get an early start myself, I pulled down my tent, packed my things, and set out to look for breakfast.

The day before, I had noticed a couple of possibilities next to the campgrounds.

While looking for a restaurant, I ran into Pilgrim and Jack, who were also hoping for a good breakfast before they hit the trail. Pilgrim suggested we three eat together, and I agreed. We found a restaurant quickly and went in and ordered. While waiting for our food, we chatted and exchanged tidbits about our lives. They were both college grads with good jobs.

After a few minutes of conversation, I took the liberty of asking them where they were spiritually. Jack said he was an atheist, happy with that, and unhappy with fundamentalist Christians in Florida, who, in his opinion, were too vocal. Pilgrim, on the other hand, admitted that she was searching for light. She said that she carried a small Bible in her pack and was reading through it on their hike.

Seizing the opportunity the Lord had provided, I shared with them several verses from Scripture concerning the salvation that God offers us through faith in His Son, Jesus Christ. As I expected, Jack did not show any interest, but Pilgrim listened attentively, and over buckwheat pancakes, we discussed what it meant to be born again and know that our sins are forgiven.

After we had finished breakfast, I thanked them for our time together. I said "good-bye" and wished them good hiking. In my heart I thanked God for the privilege of being His witness. There is no experience on earth quite like it. I had no doubt that God had brought Pilgrim, Jack, and me together to discuss life's most important question.

The weather that day turned out to be nasty—cold, windy, and raining. On the summit of Bluff Mountain, I came upon a small stone monument dedicated to a boy named Little Ottie. In spite of the miserable weather, I stopped to read the story of this little boy. He was not quite five years old when he wandered from his home in the mountains and perished. When they found his body five months later, in April of 1891, the little fellow was still wearing his cap. Parents and friends raised the memorial on the spot where he had fallen.

I was moved by the thought of Little Ottie lying down to die and being taken up to heaven in the arms of Jesus. He had wandered from home, but the Good Shepherd was watching over him. I thanked God for that little boy and for the significance of his short life in God's mysterious plan.

It was still raining when I arrived at Punch Bowl Shelter that evening at 8:30 P.M. It was rare for me to hike that late, but the long daylight hours made it possible. I had hoped to stay in a dry shelter that night, but twenty Boy Scouts and their leaders had arrived ahead of me and were settled into the shelter and nearby tents. The scout leaders offered to make space for me, for which I was grateful, but as a former scout, I knew only too well the noise a bunch of boys can make at night. So I politely declined, found a spot near Punch Bowl Pond, and set up my tent. I slept so well that night that even the croaking of the frogs in the pond didn't keep me awake.

By the next morning, the rain had diminished to a drizzle. Not eager to venture out into a wet world, I slept in an extra hour. I finally awoke when I heard a scout leader yelling to one of the boys, "Andy, get movin'. Your Ma ain't here to take care of you. You've gotta pack that stuff yourself. You wanted to hike the Appalachian Trail!" Although Andy was whining in the background, he was learning important lessons that would one day help him become a man. Thank God for the Boy Scouts!

After reading my Bible, praying, and writing in my journal, I poked my head outside the tent and happily noted that the rain had stopped. By the time I'd eaten breakfast, packed up my wet tent, and taken photos of Punch Bowl Pond, it was almost noon. This was one of my latest starts.

At 1:00, as I came out of the cold mist of the forest to a road crossing, I noticed a man and woman standing beside a van on the side of the road. To my surprise, as I passed the couple, they offered me a cinnamon bun and a glass of juice. They said they were the Williamses and they did this sort of thing every weekend in the summer. I thanked them warmly for their kindness and took their photo before I moved on. It was a dreary day, and the Trail Angels' refreshments were just what I needed. That was not the last time I would see the Williamses.

On May 25, a beautiful day, I hiked over the bald of Virginia's Cold Mountain and then hiked for miles along a splendid mountain stream. The guidebook said this was Iroquois country. Romanticist that I am, I imagined Iroquois Indians 300 years ago treading the same path that I was following, along the same rushing stream.

"Fantastic," I said to the wind as I hiked along.

Several days later, the Lord provided water in an unusual way. The weather had turned hot and dry, and through a miscalculation, I had missed a spring and found myself seriously out of water. Both of my bottles were empty, and I still had five miles to go—a long distance when you're hiking on a hot day—before reaching the next source of water. About a mile down the trail, I noticed a gallon jug tied to a tree. The jug was full of water, and attached to it was a note that read: "From Grumpy. Enjoy." What unusual ways God answers prayer! Thanking the Lord and Grumpy, I filled one of my bottles and left the rest of the water for the next thirsty hiker.

At the summit of Maintop Mountain, my poor sense of direction did me in . . . again. I became disoriented and started hiking down the mountain I just had hiked up! I was halfway down before realizing I was heading south instead of north. Not only had I lost thirty minutes of hiking time, but also I suffered a bruised ego. Although hiking in the wrong direction would happen to me several times during my months on the AT, I was fortunate it didn't happen more often. (My sense of direction is so bad that when we're driving and we come to a crossroad and my instinct tells me to turn right, my wife and I know with absolute certainty that we should turn left. It has become a standing joke with us.)

Montebello, Virginia, was near the trail, so I decided to stop at a bed and breakfast there. I hitched a ride to the B&B, but I as got out of the car and started walking to the front door, a woman leaned out a window and yelled, "No room."

So that was that. Seeing my predicament, my kind benefactors in the car offered to shuttle me to where I could find lodging. I didn't know the area, but I asked them to take me to a campground I had noticed a couple of miles back.

Arriving at the campground, I got out of the car and thanked the folks again for their help. After they drove off, I walked over to the campground—and found it closed, empty of people. I couldn't believe it; campgrounds don't close! Then I surmised it was probably too early in the season.

As I stood outside the campsite, trying to figure out what to do, a van pulled alongside of me. Inside were the Trail Angels, the Williamses, who had provided me with juice and a cinnamon roll at the road crossing two days before. Without any hesitation, they said I could stay overnight at their home a few miles away. Could God's timing be any better?

That night, I stayed with Ed and Mary Williams. Their house in the country was modest, but their generosity was elegant. They served me turkey and stuffing, left over from a Memorial Day family get-together the day before. I learned that Ed did metal work at home and Mary was a school secretary. In their free time, they helped hikers and engaged in other good works. The generosity of Ed and Mary Williams was yet another example of the good hearts of Americans.

WATCH FOR THE CRIMINAL AND THE COUGAR!

As Ed drove me back to the AT the next morning, he told me that a criminal was on the loose. He added that it was terrible that hikers were not informed of threats like that. The police wouldn't say what the criminal had done, but he was last seen in Front Royal and heading south on the AT. Ed gave me the man's description: he was six-foot two, had a red beard, and carried a green pack. I promised Ed that I would be cautious and on the lookout for anyone fitting that description. And if that wasn't enough to think about, I had seen a report on the local TV that a 100 pound cougar was prowling around in the woods. Ah, the joy of returning to the wilderness and communing with nature!

Ed wished me luck as I got out of the car, probably thinking I would need it. I gave him ten dollars, which was very little for all that he and Mary had done for me. He thanked me and said the money would be used to help other hikers in need.

Only minutes after leaving Ed, it began raining heavily. With no other choice, I put on my rain gear and plodded on in the downpour. Soon, Harpers Creek Shelter came into sight. It was off to my left about twenty yards from the trail on a hill that sloped down slightly. Thinking it would be nice to get out of the rain, I was about to turn into the shelter, when I spotted him—a tall man with a beard. From my distant cover of dripping trees, I couldn't tell if his beard was red, but his pack definitely looked green.

What should I do? I asked myself as I stood under the trees with water dripping off my nose, down my poncho, and into my soggy hiking boots. As desperately as I wanted to get out of the rain, I hesitated. What if this was the bad guy? The man hadn't seen me, so I was still safe. I decided to keep it that way. After taking a longing look at the shelter, I continued silently down the muddy trail.

I was still mulling over my decision ten minutes later when a hiker breezed by me at a good clip. He was young, tall, had a beard, and carried a green pack—the man I'd seen in the shelter! But when he said cheerfully, "Have a good hike," before disappearing down the trail, laughing at myself and my overactive imagination, I thought: *So much for the desperate criminal!*

I arrived at Maupin Shelter at 4:00 that afternoon and immediately changed into dry clothes and prepared a bowl of chicken soup. There is nothing like a bowl of hot cream of chicken soup on a cold, rainy day. As I ate, another hiker arrived. He was a distinguished-looking man in his late sixties with a gray goatee. He said his name was Gustaf and he came from Quebec.

At the mention of Quebec, I began to speak French to him. He replied in French and seemed happy to find a hiker who spoke his language. I was just as happy for the chance to speak French, which is music to my ears. Often, though, I have difficulty understanding French Canadians because of their strong accent. By contrast, however, Gustaf spoke perfect Parisian French. He was a university professor and was taking a break to hike the AT from Quebec to Georgia.

That evening, I looked for an opportunity to talk to my new friend about the Lord, but none presented itself. Gustaf's sleeping bag was near mine, and as we chatted before drifting off to sleep I said, "Gustaf, *est-ce que cela vous arrive de penser a l'éternité?*" (Do you ever think about eternity?). I added, "You know, someday we're all going to die. What then?" He had a puzzled look on his face and replied with a typically French response, "Why then, nothing. We cease to exist. We go into the ground and are absorbed into nature, into the universe, like the trees, like the plants, like everything."

France is not known as the cradle of humanism for nothing. Beginning with René Descartes, going through Voltaire, and reaching a crescendo in the French Revolution, France's philosophical thinking has eliminated divine revelation, making that country one of the most atheistic in the world. For the average French person, religion has no relationship to reality.

I quoted Hebrews 9:27 in French to Gustaf: "It is appointed unto man once to die, and after that, the judgment."

Earlier, Gustaf had remarked about his surprise at seeing so many Bibles in shelters. His education notwithstanding, he evidenced little knowledge of the Bible. In fact, his mind seemed hermetically closed to Bible truth.

Despite Gustaf's unbelief, I was convinced that there is no barrier the French can build that Christ cannot penetrate. I felt certain that the Holy Spirit would use my simple witness in Gustaf's life. My heart went out to this learned gentleman, and I prayed that his eyes might be opened to the God who created him and who loves him so much that He gave His Son to die for his sins that he might inherit eternal life. I continue to pray for Gustaf.

Chapter 13

American History
Interlude

But those who wait on the Lord shall renew their strength.
—Isaiah 40:31

Maupin Shelter to Harpers Ferry, West Virginia

I was now hiking in the Shenandoah National Park, which the trail
book described as "a delightfully wild, seventy-five-mile segment of
the Blue Ridge Mountains in Virginia." I agreed with the description:
hiking in Shenandoah was indeed delightful and not very difficult.
I decided that it would be a great place for seniors with little hiking
experience to get a taste of the Appalachian Trail. In addition, there is
lodging for hikers who are not into backpacking, with an eight-mile
day hike between lodges. I promised myself to return some day to
hike in the Shenandoahs with my wife (which we did in 2008).

Several miles before Big Meadows Lodge, I came across a small sign
pointing to Hoover Camp, which was not far off the trail. Sensing it
might be an interesting visit, I decided to follow the side trail.

I covered the distance to Hoover Camp quickly and, to my surprise,
arrived at a scene that looked like a disaster area. Several trees were down,
and the camp was circled by yellow emergency tape. It was evident that
the area had been hit hard by a severe ice-storm that had done a considerable amount of damage.

There was a spooky feeling to the place: not a soul was around, and a sign said it was closed to the public because of the danger posed by damaged trees. Telling myself that AT hikers were not "the public" and we were used to falling trees, I slipped under the yellow tape and began exploring Hoover Camp.

I had heard of a camp built by Herbert Hoover when he was president, but that's all I knew. Fortunately, there were plaques that told the history of this camp and how it had been built. Hoover Camp was the forerunner of Camp David, built during the Eisenhower years and so popular with recent presidents.

I learned Hoover camp was built in 1929 as a retreat for President Hoover from the pressures of Washington. It became a place for entertaining prime ministers and celebrities such as Charles Lindberg. There were several large, rustic buildings to house Hoover and his guests. The largest, called the "The Town House," had two huge stone fireplaces, one at each end of the building. The place was locked of course, but there was enough sun that day to allow me to see the interior by peering through a window. A sign said that Hoover would often stand before a roaring fire in the evenings and regale his guests with stories of his travels around the world. By looking through the window, it was easy for me to imagine the lively moments that had taken place in that large room.

At the back of the building I discovered a wooden deck large enough for forty or fifty people. Flowing alongside the deck was the Rapidan, a fast flowing stream. The building and deck were located there for two reasons. First, they allowed Hoover to practice his passion for trout fishing. Secondly, which I found intriguing, famous people—diplomats, ambassadors, and the like—held secret talks on that deck because the noise from the rushing stream would drown out their conversations, preventing curious ears from hearing what was said.

For me, however, the most fascinating part of Hoover Camp was a quarter-mile footpath called the "The President's Walk," on which the president enjoyed walking and talking with his guests. The narrow trail passed over a small stone bridge and into the woods adjacent to the camp. It was just a short, fifteen-minute walk, but I thought of all the crucial matters that must have been discussed on that path. The fates of nations, no doubt, had been decided while Hoover and England's prime minister, among others, strolled that path.

Feeling the historical significance, I walked over the small bridge and took a dozen steps on the trail before fallen trees blocked my way. That was enough, however, for me to taste a bit of history.

One of my goals in hiking the AT was to rediscover America. In the thirty-three years I had lived in France, I had lost touch with my own country. Visiting places like Hoover Camp gave me opportunity to touch base with scenes that figured prominently in the life of America. My little side-trail experience had been rewarding, and feeling satisfied, I shouldered my pack and took the blue-blaze trail back to the AT.

One experience that had eluded me so far was sighting a bear. I had hiked almost a thousand miles but had seen neither hide nor hair of a bear. To be truthful, I did not want to come face-to-face with a bear of any size, but catching a glimpse of one would have been nice, if for no other reason than to tell friends who often asked if I had seen any bears.

Bears were far from my mind as I sat on the trail in northern Virginia, meditating on Romans chapter 7 on that cold, cloudy morning. Suddenly I heard a loud noise about twenty yards to my right. Then a large animal came crashing out of the woods, crossed the AT, and plunged into the trees on the other side. It all happened so quickly that I saw only the back side of what appeared to be a bear disappearing into the forest. I can't say with one hundred percent certainty that it was a bear, but ninety percent was enough for me; I quickly gathered my things and left the scene. I'd gotten my glimpse, and that was enough.

Studies have shown that introverts are more likely to hike the whole AT. As somewhat of a loner, I enjoyed the solitude of the trail, but I also appreciated the friends I'd made. A day after the bear incident, I was hiking the trail near Hogback Mountain when I saw a woman headed south coming toward me.

As she drew near, she stopped and said, "I know you!" Sure enough, she did. It was Swamp Yankee, the wife of Forward March, who I had met on the trail in 1996.

We greeted each other like old friends. She reminded me that she had left the trail shortly after I last saw them in 1996 because of an injured foot. But she had not given up her dream of hiking the whole trail.

When she recovered, she "flip-flopped"; that is, she flew up north to Katahdin and started hiking south. Her husband already had finished his hike, and she was only a hundred miles or so from becoming a two-thousand miler herself.

She explained that to make it easier on her foot, she had lightened her pack to thirty pounds by chucking her stove, pots, and pans. For calories, she carried only dry mixes, such as high-protein milkshakes used by bodybuilders. Her only hot meals were those she had in trail towns once or twice a week.

I gave her the news of my progress toward Maine and then congratulated her for her determination and grit. Then we parted, Swamp Yankee hiking south and I heading north, both of us feeling the warm encouragement of having met a friend.

I spent the night at Gravel Springs Shelter. My best memory there was my great night's sleep. I never had slept so well in all my life, and I awoke after nine hours feeling gloriously refreshed. Later I noted in my journal that my sleep that night had been "delicious"—the only word that could describe it. Many times since my return to civilization, I have longed for the deep sleep I experienced on the trail.

The next day, after a six-mile hike, I reached Route 55 and hitched a ride to Front Royal, Virginia, and got a room at a Super 8 motel. After a shower and supper, I called my wife and then my son Mark to make arrangements for him to drive from his home in Harrisburg, Pennsylvania, to pick me up in Harpers Ferry the next day.

The temperature of my "Harpers Ferry fever" was rising as I neared the halfway mark. That might have explained why I didn't sleep well that night. Or it might have been because I had grown so used to sleeping in the open on hard ground or a shelter floor that I was no longer comfortable in a motel bed.

I had no trouble hitching a ride back to the trail the next morning. The man who stopped to pick me up was young and friendly and said his name was David. He was a businessman. When I noticed the large Bible on the seat between us, I knew I was in good company. David and I had some good fellowship in the Lord during our brief time together. As I thanked him for the ride and waved good-bye, I was grateful once again for the believers the Lord had sent along my hike to encourage me.

Half-way Harpers Ferry

I arrived at Harpers Ferry on June 13, 1998. Given that this was a big moment, I was surprised that I was not more jubilant. I suspected that the reason was fatigue; I was beat from too many fifteen- and sixteen-mile days, and I just dragged the last nine miles to Harpers Ferry. From experience, I knew my enthusiasm would return with a good rest and some good food.

The food problem was solved when I had a large lunch of spaghetti and meatballs at King's Pizza in Harpers Ferry. On the strength of that nourishment, I walked to a KOA campground on the edge of town that offered free showers to hikers. If I was going to meet son Mark and daughter-in-law Brandy at the post office at 6:00, I didn't want them seeing me in the condition I was in after almost forty days and forty nights in the wilderness.

I showered, shaved, and put on clean clothes. While walking around the campgrounds with my pack, several people surprised me by asking how my AT hike was going. I began to feel like a celebrity. They looked wistfully at my pack, trekking poles, and boots. These people traveled in motor homes that cost hundreds of thousands of dollars, but I think deep in their hearts many of them wished they too could walk the Appalachian Trail. I was humbled that God was giving me the strength and opportunity to do that very thing.

I walked from the campground to the center of Harpers Ferry, where I located the post office. A few minutes after six, my son's car wheeled around the corner and came to a stop in front of me. Our lovely daughter-in-law, Brandy, was beside him.

We had a happy reunion. Before we left, Brandy took a photo of me standing in full hiking gear next to the Harpers Ferry welcome sign. It was indeed a moment to remember. I had hiked a thousand miles since Springer Mountain in Georgia and had now reached the AT halfway point. We celebrated the occasion by dining at a fine restaurant just outside of Harpers Ferry. It was an excellent meal and a happy memory. On the drive to Harrisburg, I settled in the soft passenger seat of my son's car, half dozing, half dreaming of all that had taken place up to this point. What an amazing adventure it had been so far.

The Appalachian Trail

Fall 1998
40.5 miles hiked

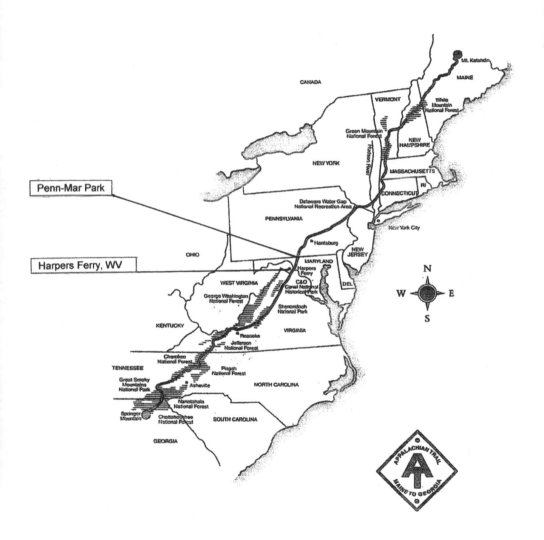

Chapter 14

Marching Through Maryland

Heirs together of the grace of life.

—1 Peter 3:7

Harpers Ferry to Pen-Mar Park

In addition to my forty-day spring trek on the AT, I was able to add another, shorter hike in the fall of 1998. Fall is my favorite season, and I knew that a hike through Maryland, the next state, would be a chance to see some autumn splendor.

An added attraction would be that my wife could accompany me. Although she gave up backpacking when our sons reached their teens, she still was walking thirty minutes a day at a pretty fast clip, so I thought she could handle a one-day hike with me if she was carrying just a light daypack. I was delighted when she agreed to my plan. She would hike the first day with me and then shuttle me on the remaining two days as I hiked through the short AT section in Maryland.

After driving to Harrisburg and spending the night with Mark and Brandy, we drove the next morning to Harpers Ferry. There we reserved a room for three nights at the Comfort Inn. Our motel room would be home base for us the next three days—the time it would take me to hike through Maryland.

There are scads of things to see in Harpers Ferry, but most interesting to us was the AT National Headquarters located there. I wanted to meet the folks who are a part of the nuts and bolts of the AT, the inner workings of the large organization called the Appalachian Trail Conference. I had talked with them numerous times on the phone, and now I would meet them personally.

The AT headquarters is modest by any standard. Its appearance models the character of the AT organization itself: low-key and unassuming, with no attempt for ostentation. The Appalachian Trail is a simple footpath, and the organization reflects that same simplicity.

Babs and I talked with several people in the office. We were given a warm welcome and made to feel that our visit was special. After we signed the register, a woman named Laurie led us outside and took our photo in front of the building so that our smiling faces would join the dozens of other hiker photos on the bulletin board. When we left the AT headquarters, I understood better the whole organization and the noble goals it seeks to accomplish.

The next morning, a shuttle driver picked us up at the appointed time and drove us north to Gathland Park, which would be the starting point for our nine-mile hike south to Harpers Ferry. My stated aim from the very beginning was always to hike north; heading south seemed to me like going backward. I wanted to keep moving onward, just like my trail name, "Onward!," which was what my fellow hikers called me. But when it came to my wife, all my rigid rules went out the window. The elevation changes hiking south would be less than those hiking north, making it easier for Babs. That was the most important consideration.

We paid the shuttle driver and started hiking. Although it was 10:40 in the morning, the air was still chilly, and I regretted that we weren't wearing gloves. However, our bodies were soon warmed from the heat that our hiking generated. Gathland Park was impressive, with many historical reminders of the Civil War. The day went as planned; there was no rain and no tough climbs, and we had good discussions. That was the best part, just talking and sharing our concerns, hopes, and dreams. Walking together in the same direction is a great way to face life.

We stopped for lunch at 1:00. After a couple hours of hiking, our whole-wheat sandwiches tasted good. Babs' knee was acting up a bit, so I showed her the exercises I used to strengthen my knees. She tried the exercises, and that seemed to help.

The hike down Weaverton Cliffs didn't seem to bother Babs' knee, and we finally arrived at the famous towpath along the Potomac River late in the afternoon. The guidebook said that as a young surveyor on horseback, George Washington had covered the same path we were on. As we walked, we discussed what America's future first president might have experienced at that point in his life. We never could know of course, but it was fun to imagine.

The next morning, Babs changed roles: no longer my hiking partner, she was now my shuttle driver. After breakfast, we drove back to Gathland Park, which had been our starting point the day before. I put on my pack and started hiking northward this time, while Babs returned to the motel for a day of study towards her master's degree in Christian counseling. With that schedule, we each worked towards our goal.

The hike through Maryland was easy; there were no big mountains, and I carried only a light daypack. The only difficulty I had was a huge boulder field that slowed my progress. Ed Garvey, the famous thru-hiker, had aptly described it as a "rocky jungle." I enjoyed the fall leaves, but I didn't find as much red as I would have liked. To me, the red fall foliage is what makes the autumn beauty so stunning.

The second day went much like the first. Our pattern was that I covered a lot of ground and then met Babs, who was waiting for me at the designated place and time. We would drive back to the motel and in the evenings, take strolls around Harpers Ferry. We finished the three days through Maryland at the lovely Pen-Mar Park, which is on the border of Maryland and Pennsylvania. The next year, 1999, I would return to this spot and continue my hike through Pennsylvania.

Before we left the park, Babs and I went over to the pavilion, held hands, and looked at a beautiful vista. A small sign on the pavilion wall said:

> Can you look at all this beauty and deny the existence of a
> loving Creator?

We could not. Our Creator-God had shown us His love in so many wonderful ways.

The Appalachian Trail

1999
530.3 miles hiked

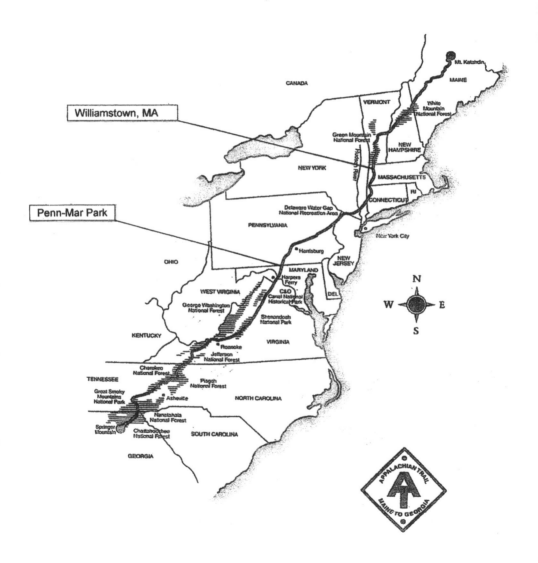

Chapter 15

Light in Duncannon Darkness

Among whom you shine as lights in the world.
—Philippians 2:14

Pen-Mar Park to Fort Dietrich Snyder

The year 1999 marked a great leap forward in my hike of the Appalachian Trail. I hiked my greatest distance on the AT up to that point, a mind-boggling 500 miles. It was hard for me to conceive of walking such a distance, but I told myself that it was just a matter of putting one foot ahead of the other—of taking a certain number of steps until I reached the goal, which on this hike was the southern border of Vermont.

I would be hiking in late summer and into the fall. With the exception of Maryland, all of my previous hikes had been in the spring. Although I loved hiking in the spring, I craved a long hike in the falling leaves, among splashes of color. The nostalgia of the fall harmonizes with my personality.

On this hike I would cover almost one-fourth of the Appalachian Trail, the closest I would come to being an actual thru-hiker. Something in me longed to respond to this challenge of walking 500 miles through the wilderness.

As always, I trained for my hike by jogging as much and as far as possible, up to two hours at a time. The first week on the trail was nevertheless rough for me, but not half as difficult as it would have been without the endurance I developed through long-distance jogging.

On the spiritual side, prayer support for my hike was growing. I had e-mailed requests for prayer to friends who shared an interest in my hike and witness on the trail; their replies were heartwarming. A prayer team was being formed, and Babs would send out regular reports to the team so that they could follow my progress. Only in heaven will I know the effectiveness of those prayers in taking me to Maine.

The beginning of my hike in Pennsylvania was near Harrisburg, Pennsylvania, where my son and his wife lived. Mark was working and in law school. Babs and I drove to their home, which would be our base of operations for the first week of my hike. From there, Babs would take me to Penn-Mar Park, my starting point, and then return to Harrisburg. During that week, she would be my shuttle driver while she enjoyed a visit with Mark and Brandy.

On the morning of August 12, 1999, Babs left me at Penn-Mar, where I began a thirteen-mile day. It was good to be back on the trail and feel the path beneath my feet. My taste for adventure was still keen, and I wondered what the next five hundred miles would hold for me.

I had walked only a hundred yards when I came to a sign that said I was crossing the Mason-Dixon Line. That was a surprise. Although I always had known of that famous border, I thought it was more a mythical designation than anything else. But there I was, standing on the dividing line between the Union and the Confederacy. I was happy with my discovery.

My first day of hiking was hot, and my shirt soon was soaked with sweat. Fortunately, even with the heat there was still water in the springs; although, in some springs the water was low. By using a cup, however, I could scoop up enough to fill my water bottles.

I was pleasantly surprised to find the shelters in the lower half of Pennsylvania to be new and well maintained, unlike the old shelters in the southern states. An old, rundown shelter could be discouraging, while a new, clean shelter could lift my spirits.

At noon the second day, I arrived at Tumbling Run Shelter and decided to take a lunch break. Another hiker was already there. He was tall, and like most hikers, thin, probably in his early twenties. He sported a ponytail and earrings. As we talked, he impressed me as being an intelligent young man, and when he told me his name was Juan Carlos, my curiosity was aroused.

Juan Carlos said his father was Spanish Basque and his mother was American. Having lived in southern France for many years, I told him I knew something about the Basque country between France and Spain and appreciated the beauty of that area.

When I turned the conversation to spiritual things, Juan Carlos was quite ready to pursue that subject as well. I offered him a tract ("Are You Going to Heaven?"), and to my surprise, he said he'd already read it. He explained that he had come across that very tract several days before while leafing through the pages of a shelter register. I was excited to learn that my tracts were being read. Certainly, the Lord had arranged this encounter with Juan Carlos.

He then told me that he had been given another gospel tract on the trail a month before. While he sat on a bench at Fontana Village, near Fontana Dam, a woman approached him, wordlessly handed him a tract, and then walked away. He had read the pamphlet and was highly offended because it had stated in no uncertain terms that he was a sinner and on his way to hell. He said, "How could this woman, who knew nothing about me and had never met me before, give me a piece of literature that says I am condemned to eternal punishment?"

On hearing that, I felt strongly that God was trying to speak to this young man. That he had been given two tracts was no accident. After quoting several Bible verses, I explained to Juan Carlos that all of us have sinned and are spiritually lost. That's the human condition, according to God. In God's eyes we are condemned. Further, I said that if we refuse to acknowledge sin and try by our own efforts to win God's favor, we will never obtain eternal life—the free gift of God through Jesus Christ.

Unfortunately, Juan Carlos rejected my explanation and replied that it was wrong to say that other religions were false. As he argued for the necessity of tolerance, I thought I was listening to a postmodernist lecture. The young man was obviously intelligent but was steeped in a philosophy completely in disagreement with God's Word. He was in darkness, light years from understanding God's provision for man's salvation. I thought of Jesus' reaction to the rich young ruler who was trying his hardest to get to heaven his own way, and Jesus looked on him and loved him.

Just then two other hikers arrived at the shelter, and our conversation came to an end. As I left Juan Carlos and resumed hiking, I thanked God for the privilege of being a small link in a chain that might someday lead to his conversion. I thought too of the woman who had given him a tract at Fontana Village, who probably was too timid and scared to say even a word. She never would know that her printed message had ignited anger in a young hiker, with a word that still burned in his consciousness. I was reminded again that no witness for Christ is ever lost or given in vain; it will always bear fruit in some form. I made a mental note to pray for Juan Carlos, which I continue to do.

The next day was relaxed. I hiked only eight miles, from Shippensville to Pine Grove Furnace Park. But those eight miles were special because I hiked them with my wife, our son Mark, and our daughter-in-law, Brandy. I had looked at my map and decided that those eight miles must be the AT's most pleasant hike. With a gentle decline all the way, it would be perfect for a short family hike.

We were on the trail by 10:15 that morning. At 1:00 we stopped for lunch at a shady campsite and basked in the lovely weather and woodland beauty. After lunch, I pulled my billed cap over my eyes, propped my back against a fallen log, and took a nap. Babs stretched out on a soft green patch of ground moss and meditated on the trees and sky. Mark and Brandy conversed softly nearby.

At 3:30 that afternoon, we reached Pine Grove Furnace Park pleasantly tired. We celebrated by buying ice cream at a snack bar located next to a building where George Washington once stayed. I sat in a comfortable chair with my ice cream, thinking that it had been a satisfying day filled with good memories that would stay with us for a long time.

When we arrived back at Mark and Brandy's house in Harrisburg, my eldest son, Chad, was waiting for us. He planned to hike the next five days with me and was excited. However, that excitement would be diminished before the five days were over.

That evening, we all went out to Ruby Tuesday for supper, and the next morning, we attended Mark and Brandy's church in Harrisburg. Brandy served us dinner after the service, and before we left for the AT, we all had a brief moment of prayer on the tree-lined sidewalk in front of their house.

It was Sunday afternoon, September 16, 1999, when Babs deposited Chad and me at Pine Grove Furnace Park. As Chad and I hiked through the park, we passed dozens of families enjoying grilled steak and fried chicken. These folks were there for a fun-filled couple of hours; but I, as a long-distance hiker, was on a difficult journey toward the Promised Land, which would take me many months.

Our big event of the day was passing the official AT midpoint marker—the real one this time. The sign said it was 1,069 miles south to Springer Mountain, Georgia, and 1,069 miles north to Katahdin, Maine. We gave a celebratory shout, and Chad took my picture as I stood in front of the halfway sign to mark the occasion.

After spending the night at Tagg Run Shelters, we hiked twelve miles the next day to Boiling Springs, Pennsylvania. Our last mile lacked the cooling canopy of foliage; but, although we hiked that leg under the hot sun, we quickly forgot our discomfort as we took in the charm of Boiling Springs. I was captivated by this shady little village with Civil War period homes and a center dominated by a lovely pond populated by mallard ducks.

Chad and I made our way to the Garmanhaus Bed and Breakfast, where we had reserved a room for the night. We parked our backpacks on an outside balcony, as the owner, John Garman, had rather forcefully insisted we do. I guessed he had problems in the past with some "wildlife" being brought into the home via the backpacks. We quickly changed our clothes and then trotted down to the local swimming pool, where we enjoyed a refreshing swim nearly all by ourselves.

Chad's enjoyment was diminished by the blisters on his feet caused by his new boots that weren't broken in, and the pool's rough bottom only aggravated the pain.

Our swim was followed by a fine meal at a local Italian restaurant. The menu reminded me that I was no longer in Virginia, and here in Pennsylvania, fried chicken had given way to spaghetti, strombolli, and pizza.

After supper we took an enjoyable stroll around Boiling Springs and then returned to our B&B. Built in 1860, Garmanhaus was big, and its beauty was enhanced by an abundance of colorful flowers in front of the house. Before we left the next morning, we asked John, the owner, to take our photo with the house and flowers as a backdrop.

The weather was cool as we hiked out of Boiling Springs, but it soon heated up, and again, we were exposed to a lot of sun. In addition, the scenery was not terribly inspiring. In places, the woods were scrubby and filled with what I call "low-class vegetation." But with hiking—as with everything in life—we had to take the bad with the good, and I knew that the beauty eventually would return.

Then, big disappointment hit us at about 6:00 that evening, when Chad announced with great reluctance that he was suffering so much from his blisters that he would have to drop out of our hike. We both felt bad about this, but when foot problems develop, you have only one option: leave the trail.

We hiked another mile and reached a main highway, where we stopped at a house to ask the owner if we could use their phone. After I called Mark, he arrived twenty minutes later to take Chad back to his car, which was parked at Mark's house. I gave Chad a hug, and he and his brother drove off.

I felt the usual twinge of sadness as my sons drove away. With a sigh, I crossed the highway and found the white blazes that marked the trail. Fortunately, I didn't have much time to brood over Chad's departure because I had to reach Darlington Shelter before nightfall. The two miles to the shelter proved to be a tough climb, and I didn't reach the shelter until after 8:00 that evening. Three other hikers were already there.

The flame from my camp stove glowed in the near-darkness as I prepared my supper, a chicken-pasta mix that Chad had given me when he left. While I cooked my meal, I talked with a southbound hiker named Dave, who was in his last year of college and wanted to work somewhere outdoors. I don't remember how we started talking about religion, but Dave said that he had abandoned the Catholic Church because it was too narrow and he thought it didn't teach the truth.

"Even the Pope has doubts," he said.

I encouraged Dave to read the Bible because "faith comes by . . . hearing the Word of God." I briefly outlined God's way of salvation and gave him a tract to follow up my explanation of the gospel.

Chad's chicken mix was delicious. But even more satisfying was the opportunity to share the Bread of Life with a young man who was seeking truth. I felt as well that this was God's way of encouraging me after Chad's departure. By 9:00, I was in my sleeping bag.

After leaving Darlington Shelter the next morning, I had another tough climb. But the day was beautiful, and I had my hiking legs back. I was again enjoying the exercise. After a rocky descent, I arrived at the trail town of Duncannon. The trail passed right through this small town that had seen better days. Some of the buildings on the main street were run down, and a few were empty. It was evident that sometime in the past Duncannon had experienced an economic downturn.

I decided to stay there in the Doyle Hotel. I had read that some of the most famous AT backpackers had stayed there over the years, and I thought perhaps there might be some reminders of AT history at the Doyle Hotel.

But my expectations fell flat. When I arrived at the hotel, the restaurant-bar in the front was closed. All that remained was an old, dilapidated building that was breathing its last. As I peered through the dirty windows of the bar and imagined what congenial meetings had taken place among hikers there in decades past, I could almost hear the rowdy laughter of long ago.

Hoping to find lodging elsewhere, I picked up my backpack to leave. Then a rather seedy-looking man approached me. He had the appearance of being either a former or present alcoholic. He said his name was Glen, and he was in charge of hotel lodging. He said I could spend the night at the hotel for $10.55. The price was right, so I said "yes," but was instantly assailed by doubts and wondered what I was getting myself into.

Glen took me into the building by a side door and then led me up a creaky staircase to the second floor. On the way up, he apologized for the chunks of plaster that had fallen from the ceiling the night before. As we sidestepped the chunks on the staircase, I was disturbed by the silence in the building. As far as I could tell, I was the only lodger at Doyle Hotel that night, and it was not a comforting thought.

Glen took me to a room down a long hallway and opened the door. I took one look around and longed for the coziness of my tent. This place was a flophouse of the first order, the picture of despair. My bedroom for the night made the average rescue mission look like the Waldorf-Astoria. Paint was peeling from the walls, and a naked light bulb hung in the middle of the room. The throw rugs on the floor were worn and dirty. Glen carried with him rumpled sheets that he put on the bed. I hoped I was the first to use them.

When I gave Glen my $10.55, I had the distinct impression that I was being ripped off. As he left, Glen showed me a padlock that I was to use, without fail, whenever I left the room. The padlock was huge, but it did little to remove my apprehensions.

The one redeeming feature of the hotel was the new shower in the bathroom, which was down the hall from my room. Putting the heavy padlock in place, I walked to the bathroom and enjoyed a hot shower. As I soaked under the steaming water, I reasoned that, though my surroundings were miserable, it was part of my AT adventure, and I decided to make the most of it.

After my shower, I dressed, put the heavy padlock in place again, and went out for something to eat. *Perhaps that will cheer my spirits,* I thought. Isn't it amazing how the prospect of a good meal can encourage a person? Especially a hungry hiker who's trying to replenish the 5,000 calories burned during the day.

It was almost dark. At first I saw nothing on the main street to lift my morale. Many downtown buildings looked neglected or abandoned. Having come from a part of Ohio that had been hit hard by the closing of steel mills, the scene was familiar. The loss of jobs and a failing economy had produced waves of despair.

Then I noticed a small storefront building with lights blazing inside, and my whole outlook changed. A sign in front of the building said "Abundant Harvest," which made me realize that this building housed an evangelical church. Through the window, I could see that the décor was simple but clean and cheerful. A small group of people stood around talking and fellowshipping. When I remembered it was Wednesday night, I realized this was a prayer meeting that had just finished.

Standing outside looking in, I thought, *A gleam of light in Duncannon darkness.* I had not been impressed with Duncannon, but God was. He loved the folks in this town so much that he had raised up a group of Christians who were praying, studying the Word, and seeking to share the gospel with friends and neighbors. That little scene changed my whole feeling about the town. God was at work in Duncannon.

I continued on down the street, where I found an Italian restaurant and consumed half of a huge strombolli. The other half would serve as lunch the next day. Encouraged, I returned to my dismal room in the hotel. I put the padlock in place, and with the help of the naked light bulb, I read from the Bible and my paperback. Then I dropped off to sleep—in my sleeping bag rather then between Glen's rumpled and suspect hotel sheets.

Before leaving Duncannon the next morning, I telephoned Babs. She felt as bad as I did about Chad's premature departure from the trail, but I assured her that it happens to the best of hikers. Following the white blazes out of town that beautiful morning down shady streets with well kept homes, I had a more favorable impression of Duncannon.

At 6:30 that evening, I rolled into the new Peter's Mountain Shelter. It was large and attractive, but to get water for my supper, I had to hike down a set of steep, stone steps to a spring. It took me a good twenty minutes going down and twenty-five to come back. One hiker had written in a register: "No wonder the water's cold—you have to go to Canada to get it!" It was a long trek, but I had only admiration for the maintenance crew that had built the stone staircase to the spring. It was a work of art and a labor of love.

Ben Franklin and Me

Eight miles into my hike the next day, I came to the site of a historical landmark, Fort Dietrich Snyder. The information I gained about the fort was a history buff's delight. A stone memorial marker explained that on that very spot, Fort Snyder had been constructed under the direction of Captain Benjamin Franklin. Its purpose was to protect settlers from Iroquois Indians during the bloody French and Indian War. I calculated that Franklin would have been in his late twenties when he oversaw the construction of the fort around 1735.

Apart from a few scattered stones here and there, I was disappointed that no trace of the fort remained. Then I noticed a sign pointing to a nearby spring. It was a hot day, and I decided to refill my water bottles. Arriving at the spring, I found another small plaque, which said that in all likelihood Ben Franklin and his men had used that very spring while constructing the fort.

I had stumbled on a direct link to the famous Ben Franklin, a man I admired for his wise influence on our nation in its early decades. The spring was located under shade trees that promised cool relief on a hot day, and I imagined Captain Franklin filling his canteen exactly as I was doing that day. As he drew his water out of the spring, Franklin would have had to keep a sharp eye out for Indians. I, however, filled my plastic Nalgene bottles with no worries for my safety.

The site was so pleasant and historic that I was tempted to linger an hour there. But the trail was calling, and I still had miles to go before the end of the day. As I resumed my hike, I prayed that God would give America men of Ben Franklin's stature in this generation.

Chapter 16

Port Clinton and the Sound of Music

Therefore, if anyone is in Christ, he is a new creation.
—2 Corinthians 5:17

Fort Snyder to Lehigh Gap, Pennsylvania

I hiked twelve miles that day and spent the night in my tent at a campsite. Early the next morning, I was on the trail and heading toward Port Clinton, Pennsylvania. As usual, the lure of a hot meal and a hot shower was pushing me on.

It would be another twelve-mile day, and so far, I hadn't encountered the infamous Pennsylvania rocks that I had heard so much about. However, the trail got rockier the closer I got to Port Clinton. As I gingerly picked my way through the rocks, I reminded myself that all it would take to scuttle my hike for that year was one little slip, on one little rock. Hikers are never more than one step from a surprise trip home.

The last mile before Port Clinton was the most challenging. I found myself on the longest, sharpest descent I had yet encountered on the trail. Instead of a backpack, I needed a parachute! My only consolation was that I was hiking down Blue Mountain and not up, which would have been even more difficult.

I was more than halfway down the long descent when I heard music that I could not immediately identify. Music in the wilderness? After a minute, I recognized that it was organ music floating up to me from somewhere. I stopped to listen, and then I recognized the old hymn "Beyond the Sunset." I hadn't heard that hymn in years.

Continuing my descent, I started singing the hymn, and the words came back to me. The fatigue and touch of loneliness I felt that day were washed away by the lovely music and encouraging words. I was dying to know where the music had come from.

I reached the base of Blue Mountain and approached the bridge that would take me into Port Clinton. Looking around, I noticed a family fishing on the banks of the Schuylkill River. To my surprise, they waved to me as if they knew me. Then the father left his fishing pole and his family and bounded up the bank to greet me. Introducing himself, he said that he had thru-hiked the AT in 1973, when he was in college.

I thought, *Once an AT hiker, always an AT hiker.* It had been more than twenty years since this man had hiked the trail, but he was still in love with it.

I congratulated the man on taking his family fishing and remarked how much it would mean to his kids when they were older. The father beamed and thanked me. I then told him how much I had enjoyed the organ music as I hiked down Blue Mountain and wondered where it had come from. He said he thought it came from a church on the other side of the river, although he didn't know which one. We reminisced for fifteen minutes about the AT before he returned to his family and I moved on.

As I crossed the bridge into Port Clinton, I remembered that as a boy Daniel Boone had camped along this very river. The Schuylkill still looked pretty wild. I thought too about the church that played hymns for the townspeople. Those Christians never would know that they had encouraged a weary backpacker that day. I concluded that much of our service for Christ is like that; we'll never know all the lives we've touched until we get to heaven. Most likely, that's the way God planned it. It reduces our temptations toward pride and increases the big surprises waiting for us when we arrive in heaven.

Chad and me at Fontana Dam, N.C., ready for a day of hiking (5/13/96)

Overmountain Shelter—a barn in N.C. transformed into an unusual
lodging place for hikers (5/22/97)

Chad and me in Pennsylvania, passing the official AT half-way marker (8/14/99)

Sunset on Mt. Lafayette in New Hampshire (8/14/2001)

Hiking Maine's Mahoosuc Notch—the AT's toughest mile. Notice the
white blazes on the rock. (8/29/2001)

The cold early morning of September 30, 2001, and Chad and I are ready to climb
Mt. Katahdin. (Babs hiked the first mile with us.)

The summit of Katahdin—to God be the glory! (9/30/2001)

Chad's moment of triumph (9/30/2001)

On the way home, Babs and I stopped in New Hampshire to climb Mt. Willard—thirty-seven years after our honeymoon! (In the background is Crawford Notch.)

Port Clinton and the Sound of Music

My first impression of Port Clinton was favorable; the town was small, and the buildings were old but well maintained. Several of the buildings were painted vivid colors, much the like the pastel tones of buildings I had seen on a visit to southern Ireland. There is nothing like splashes of color to brighten the drabness.

I found my way to the local hotel, which was easy to do in a small town. My reception at the hotel, however, was not as friendly as my encounter with the family fishing on the river. A sign on the hotel front door warned hikers to leave their backpacks outside, out of respect for other guests. The place didn't appear very hiker-friendly.

I took off my pack and pushed my way into the bar, which was dark and heavy with the usual cigarette smoke. The woman at the bar eyed me suspiciously and asked to see my driver's license when I inquired about a room. Did I look like a derelict, or had she had problems with hikers in the past? I didn't hold the woman's attitude against her; there were a few rude hikers out there. I thought that perhaps as a Christian, I could make a favorable impression.

After paying for my room, I retrieved my pack from the porch and lugged it up a wooden staircase to the second floor. I found room number two, which included two single beds, a minuscule TV, and a window fan. It wasn't exactly the Holiday Inn, but for $27.50 I wouldn't complain.

The woman at the bar had warned me that they stopped serving supper at 7:45, so I set my pack on the floor, washed my hands, and hurried downstairs. Sitting on a high stool at the bar, I ordered a veal cutlet and a baked potato with lots of butter. I was already salivating at the thought of a hot meal.

While I waited for my order, a bearded man with a ponytail, who was seated on the stool next to me, began plying me with questions about the AT. I was used to these questions by now and tried to answer them as well as I could. The man, about forty, said that he once seriously had considered hiking the AT, but that was before age and arthritis had caught up with him. Now, because work was scarce, he'd been thinking of striking out with his truck and camper to discover the back roads of America. I told him I thought that was a great idea and wished him all the best in his adventure.

I gave him a tract, which he looked over. Pushing the tract into his shirt pocket and promising to read it later, he said, "My mother was a Cherokee, and I'm a follower of Native American religion." He added, "Now, I wouldn't say I'm not a Christian, but I believe in the earth."

I replied that loving the earth was fine, but it was more important to know the One who created the earth and that it was possible to know Him through a personal relationship with His Son, Jesus Christ. We talked for a few minutes until my supper arrived. He wished me good luck on my hike as he climbed down from the barstool and headed toward the door. Bowing my head, I thanked the Lord for the food. I also prayed for the man I just had talked to, that the Holy Spirit might use the brief witness I had given him. Then I attacked my veal cutlet with the gusto of a famished lumberjack.

When I left Port Clinton the next morning, my pack was heavier with the groceries I had purchased, but my heart was lighter. I now knew an Appalachian Trail enthusiast who took his family fishing and a Native American who had a gospel tract in his pocket. And I had been cheered by a song that reminded me that the best was yet to come—beyond the sunset.

At the end of my first day out of Port Clinton, I arrived at a shelter after an easy hike of 6.3 miles. It rained heavily all that night, and ensconced in my warm sleeping bag the next morning, I said a groggy, sincere, "Wonderful!" It hadn't rained in a long time, and I was afraid that the springs would soon dry out. With a heavy rain pounding on the shelter roof, I knew that water along the trail now would be abundant.

I hiked nine miles to Ekkville Shelter, and to my amazement, the last five had been rock-free. By now I had grown so used to rocks on the trail that I almost had forgotten what it was like to hike without them.

In a meadow that day, I met a nine-year-old boy. He asked me if I had seen an older woman, his grandmother, on the trail. She evidently was somewhere in the vicinity. The boy was unusually friendly and mature for his age. He then told me that his grandmother's trail name was Bible-Thumper, and he added, "She is a *real* Christian."

I chuckled at the boy's openness and sincere admiration for his grandmother and told him that, although I would enjoy meeting his grandmother, I had a lot of miles to hike that day.

A Highway to Heaven

Midway through the next morning, I came upon a man doing trail maintenance. I appreciated the amazing work that trail maintainers did and expressed my thanks to them whenever I had the opportunity. This man, whom I judged to be around fifty, said his trail name was Skywalker. He had hiked the AT in Pennsylvania three times and hoped someday to do the whole AT, from Georgia to Maine.

We chatted several minutes about the beauty of the trail. As I left Skywalker, I handed him a tract that explained how to get to heaven. He thanked me and said, "I've been thinking about this."

I should have picked up on that comment and questioned him further, but I didn't. As I continued hiking, I felt bad about my failure to pursue our conversation. I told the Lord that if I met the man again, I would ask him about his relationship with God.

God heard me, and sure enough, when I stopped for a break at Allentown Shelter four miles down the trail, Skywalker was there. He was sawing some branches and seemed glad to see me again. I took off my pack and sat on the steps of the shelter, which was new and a model of rustic beauty.

I remembered my promise to witness to this man, but again I hesitated—this time because a tall young man, a southbound hiker named Fox Trot, was sitting on the steps of the shelter. Fox Trot was friendly, but when I talk to someone about their soul, I prefer it to be one-on-one.

Fox Trot gave no indication of leaving, and I realized that if I was going to talk to Skywalker about spiritual matters, it would have to be now or never. Farther down the trail, I would learn that God had a reason for Fox Trot being there.

I asked Skywalker about his interest in heaven. He stopped cutting branches and set his saw down. He replied that he had been thinking seriously about how to be right with God.

So, with Fox Trot listening beside me, I explained to Skywalker God's plan of salvation and how we could know for sure that our sins are forgiven. I could tell that God was speaking to Skywalker; I saw on his face intense interest and spiritual hunger.

I talked for another fifteen minutes, and when I finished, Skywalker said his car was parked at a road crossing two miles up the trail. Could we continue our conversation as we walked there together? I readily agreed.

Skywalker and I said "good-bye" to Fox Trot and walked down the trail, Skywalker with his saw over his shoulder and I with my pack on my back. He told me about his troubled conscience and his search for peace with God, which had been ongoing for years.

I listened to him, convinced that God was speaking to him. And, like Bunyan's Pilgrim, Skywalker was longing to get rid of his burden of sin. When he finished, I recounted how Christ had come into my life and what he had done for me.

After walking slowly for thirty minutes, we came in sight of his car. We were almost at the car when Skywalker stopped, turned to me, and asked, "Can you tell me how I can let God come into my life?"

His question sounded a lot like the Philippian jailor's "What must I do to be saved?" I took off my pack and then took out my Bible and showed Skywalker several verses from the New Testament. I explained how he could receive God's gift of salvation in Christ.

He read the verses out loud, and when I asked him if he was ready to take Christ as his Savior, he said without hesitation, "Yes."

We stood with our heads bowed in the middle of the path as Skywalker confessed that he was a sinner and asked in simple words for Christ to come into his life and save him. That day, August 18, 1999, the Appalachian Trail became a highway to heaven.

After we prayed, the wide smile on Skywalker's face told me that his burden was gone. He knew that his sins were forgiven. Like the Ethiopian eunuch in Acts, Skywalker went on his way rejoicing. As he drove off, he laid on the horn, giving a metallic version of the Hallelujah Chorus.

When I pulled on my forty-pound pack, it felt light as a feather, and I lifted my heart in praise to God for what the Holy Spirit had just accomplished. Never had the trail looked so beautiful. Never had I felt so refreshed and so enthusiastic about my hike. The Lord was making known His salvation on the Appalachian Trail. He was using a weak and often fearful Christian to witness in the wilderness about His love and power.

But the events of that meeting had another and unexpected impact. Four days later, I stopped at the Leroy A. Smith shelter for a lunch break, and as I often did, I read the shelter log while munching a sandwich. To my surprise, I discovered an entry written by Fox Trot, the young man hiking south who had been sitting next to me as I explained the gospel to Skywalker four days earlier.

In neatly written script, Fox Trot told a sad story. He had left the trail two weeks earlier for home, to attend the funeral of his father, who had been killed in a tragic accident. While there, Fox Trot received the news that his best friend had died of cancer. The final crushing blow came when he learned that his girlfriend had left for California with another man. These were the burdens he brought back with him when he returned to the trail after the funeral. The young man ended the entry with words that still haunt me: "There are days on the trail when the heaviest thing I carry is my heart."

Now I understood why Fox Trot sat on the steps of the Allentown Shelter as I explained God's plan of salvation to Skywalker. God had put that hurting young man there to hear a message of hope. I don't know what God did in Fox Trot's heart that day, but I do know that God moves in mysterious ways. I'm looking forward someday to learning "the rest of the story."

TOUGH CLIMB OUT OF LEHIGH GAP

Two days after my experience with Skywalker, I arrived at Lehigh Gap, Pennsylvania. Standing at the bottom of the gap and looking up at the mass of rock above, I felt intimidated. I never had done much rock climbing, but I could tell that today I would learn more about that sport.

I started climbing and made good progress until I reached a ledge that was simply too steep. If I tried it with my heavy pack on, I would risk toppling over backward. Then I had an idea. I took off my pack and, with considerable effort, hoisted it to the higher ledge. Then I climbed up after it. Fortunately, there were no experienced hikers around to laugh at my clumsy climbing. I didn't dare look down, but when finally I reached the top of the mountain, I looked back at where I'd come from and thanked the Lord for His help.

Despite the cliffhanger at Lehigh Gap, the hike through Pennsylvania was going well. The rocks had been troublesome, but not as bad as all the stories I'd heard. Now there remained only thirty-five miles between me and Delaware Water Gap, where I would leave Pennsylvania and enter New Jersey.

Chapter 17

Pond of Dreams

The earth is full of the goodness of the Lord.

—Psalm 33:5

Lehigh Gap to Dennytown Campsite

Wednesday, September 1, 1999, I was again on a roll. The hiking that morning was relatively easy, and I hoped to be in Delaware Water Gap by noon. This was the first time I would knock off 500 miles in one section hike, and I was lovin' it.

An amusing incident happened that morning. I'd stopped at a road crossing to check my maps when a car passed. Then it stopped suddenly and backed up to where I was standing, and a well-dressed woman holding a camera hopped out and came running over to me.

She explained that she had read about the Appalachian Trail and was fascinated by it. Further, she was a member of a women's club and wanted to show her friends a photo of a real, live AT hiker. Could she take my photo? I was anything but photogenic with my three-day beard and uncombed hair. But the woman was so enthusiastic that I couldn't refuse her request.

She took my photo, thanked me profusely, and hopped back into her expensive-looking car. As she and her husband drove off, I chuckled as I thought of my photo being passed around and admired by the members of her garden—or was it her yacht?—club. Clearly, I mused, I was on my way to becoming a hero among the rich and famous!

Ah, but a haughty spirit goes before a fall! Later that morning, my scrambled sense of direction did me in again. Somehow, before I reached Delaware Water Gap, I got confused and hiked an hour in the wrong direction before realizing that I was walking south instead of north. A trail sign finally awakened me to my embarrassing error. Talk about a deflated ego.

Delaware Gap is a pleasant little town. I had no trouble finding the hiker hostel, which was located in the basement of the Presbyterian Church of the Mountain. The facilities at the hostel were more than adequate, with bunk beds, a hot shower, free towels, and a lounge.

Heeding the sign in the bathroom, "Short showers. Water is scarce," I showered quickly, dressed, and then went to the post office for my general delivery mail. Just seeing my wife's handwriting on one of the envelopes brightened my day. After reading her letter, I thought of her love as I strolled two blocks to the Dinner Gap Restaurant, which had been recommended to me by another hiker.

The restaurant was a hiker's paradise: huge amounts of delicious food at reasonable prices. I ordered the stuffed pork chops with all the trimmings, which was almost more than I could handle. This was one of the few times on my hike that I met my match at mealtime, and I was not able to finish the dessert, an exquisite bread pudding.

Following that feast, I returned to the hostel. The sun was low on the horizon as I relaxed in a lawn chair under fir trees in front of the Church of the Mountain. I sat on a grassy knoll that sloped gently toward the quiet street. A mild breeze blew softly over me as I thanked the Lord for the day, and even for my lousy sense of direction.

Then I pulled out the paperback that I carried on this hike, the biography of D. L. Moody. As I read, I marveled at how God had taken a young man with few apparent abilities (at age twenty he could barely read) and made him the great evangelist of the nineteenth century. Moody was living proof that God delights in using losers to accomplish mighty things. Little is much when God is in it. I finished reading and was much encouraged. I retired for the night.

The next morning I awoke with extraordinary enthusiasm because in a few miles, I would enter my eighth state—New Jersey. The first natural phenomenon I would come across in New Jersey was Sunfish Pond, a lake that held special significance to me.

But first I had to hike out of Delaware Water Gap. As I walked along a lovely, well-graded trail, I thought again of Earl Shaffer, who in 1948 became the first person to solo hike the whole Appalachian Trail. Earl had served his country in the Pacific in WWII, and I suspect he was trying to walk out the painful memories of his war experience on the AT.

Shaffer recounts in his book that while hiking out of Delaware Water Gap he met a distinguished-looking man with a cane, out for a stroll on a sunny afternoon. The elderly gentleman wore a suit, white shirt, and tie. He and Shaffer fell into friendly conversation. In the course of their chat the man quoted from Acts 2:19:

> Your young men shall see visions and your old men shall dream dreams.

The elderly man paused and said, "That's why I come here . . . to dream dreams."

That gentleman expressed an important truth: no matter what our age, as Christians, we never should stop dreaming. As long as we're on earth there are mountains to climb, discoveries to be made, adventures to live. And the Appalachian Trail is a great place for dreamers.

I was still hiking out of the gap when, once again, I became the AT poster boy. A man and woman, about my age and out for a walk, stopped me. The woman looked me up and down, noting my backpack, sweatband, hiking poles, hiking shorts, gaiters, and boots, and exclaimed, "Well, you are the *real* thing, aren't you?"

For a second, I wasn't sure what she meant. Then I realized that because of my hiking gear, she had concluded that I was an authentic Appalachian Trail hiker, maybe the first one she had ever met. I gave this lady the only answer that came to mind: "Yes, ma'am, I guess I am."

Once again I was impressed by the aura of adventure and romance that surrounds the Appalachian Trail in the minds of many Americans.

Having felt the same awe about AT hikers decades before, I understood the woman's feelings perfectly.

I said "good-bye" to Pennsylvania and crossed into New Jersey, state number eight on my hike. Crossing a new state line always gave me a fresh shot of adrenalin because it represented a significant step toward the goal of reaching Maine.

A few miles later, I reached Sunfish Pond. Years before, when reading about this pristine glacial lake in the guidebooks, I noted where it was on my AT map and concluded that if I could reach Sunfish Pond, I would be assured of going the whole distance. This wasn't a logical conclusion, but rather something my mind cooked up to encourage me. Nevertheless, Sunfish Pond became an important milestone along my journey toward Katahdin.

This pond became a symbol that fueled my dreams when I was in France planning my expedition. Near our home in the suburbs of Bordeaux was a small wooded area where I would often go to pray. At one end of the woods was a tiny pond inhabited by a few frogs. As I prayed about hiking the AT, that little pond became Sunfish Pond in my imagination. Standing before that little pool of water, I believed that someday I would reach the real Sunfish Pond . . . and eventually Maine.

At the southern end of the pond, I came to a wooden sign that read simply: "Sunfish Pond." And there it was, in all its shining splendor, as beautiful as I had imagined for so long. The lovely autumn day created the perfect backdrop for my first glimpse of Sunfish Pond as the sun shimmered on the surface of its blue water. A long-standing prayer was being answered.

I continued walking along the rocky shore of the pond, admiring it and taking photos. Because it was noon, I stopped at a quiet spot on the water's edge to eat my lunch and meditate. What a glorious day to kick back and remember all of God's goodness in allowing me to "dream dreams."

That evening I reached Mohican Camp Center, where I was pleased to learn that my overnight stay, including a hot shower, was free of charge. But even that good news was surpassed by the sign outside the office informing me that I had hiked 1,227 miles since Georgia. I was only 882 miles from Katahdin! I put up my little tent and slept well that night.

THE BURNING BUSH

By 6:30 P.M. the next day, I was only a mile from Brink Road Shelter, where I'd planned to spend the night. But as I hiked over Rattlesnake Mountain, which overlooked Wallpack Valley, I spied a level stretch of open meadow that looked perfect for setting up my tent and decided to camp there for the night instead.

That decision was providential because later as I was bent over my gas stove preparing supper, I happened to look up at the sky—and almost knocked over my cooking pot! The sky was aflame with one of the most beautiful sunsets I ever had seen.

Supper was forgotten as I raced for my camera. Knowing that the awesome sunset would last only minutes, I snapped a half-dozen photos. Then I walked around that little stretch of open meadow, overwhelmed with the glory of God being unveiled before my very eyes. I was Moses before the burning bush. Tasting heaven and ever longing for more, I shouted and wept as God bathed me in His mighty love in those glorious moments.

I ate a late supper that night, but it didn't matter. My soul was filled with something infinitely more satisfying than beef stroganoff. If I had been harboring doubts about reaching Katahdin, they were gone. And as I crawled into my tent and then into my sleeping bag, I felt at peace. Assured that the same God who had just revealed His glory to me would take me all the way to Maine, I drifted off to sleep.

While hiking north the next morning, I passed Brink Road Shelter and thanked the Lord for leading me to camp on top of Rattlesnake Mountain. Had I spent the night at the shelter, I would have missed the "out-of-this-world" experience the night before.

BAD NIGHT AT BACKTRACK

As in life, there are ups and downs on the AT. One of my down experiences happened in Uniontown, New York, on September 6, 1999, which happened to be Labor Day. I was still in New Jersey, but the trail at one point meandered over the New York State line and into the town of Unionville, where, according to the trail guide, there was an inexpensive hostel. Because I needed to resupply, I decided to head to Unionville.

It was almost dark when I reached the side trail that led into town. About a mile from my destination, it started to rain. And making matters worse, the batteries in my flashlight gave out (again!). I didn't carry extra batteries because of the weight, so I was forced to follow the trail by my instincts. Praying that I would not lose my way or take a nasty fall in the dark, I strained to see the blazes on trees, grateful that they were white. At last I reached Lott Road, which led into town, I breathed a sigh of relief. A few streetlights told me I was on the outskirts of Unionville.

The rain was falling more heavily now, and I was wet in spite of my rain gear. As I trudged, wet and weary, down a street in the darkness to the center of town, I passed a home that had a large picture window. Through the window I could see a family of eight or nine people gathered around the supper table, eating, laughing, and enjoying themselves. The warmth of that family setting, framed by the picture window, made the dark dampness of my situation seem all the more depressing. They were in a cozy home, and I was in the street; they were with family, and I was alone. I thought of all the street people, the homeless, who for a multitude of reasons are always on the outside looking in. That lonely night I could, in a small way, identify with the homeless. It gave me a new perspective of their plight.

Soon I reached the center of town, but I saw no sign of a hostel. As I stood there, bedraggled in the driving rain, a police cruiser drove by slowly. The two officers inside the cruiser eyed me suspiciously.

Great, I thought, *all I need now is to get picked up for vagrancy!*

Then the police car stopped and an officer rolled down his window.

Trying to let them know I was a respectable hiker and not a drifter, I asked them where I could find the Backtrack Inn, where the hiker hostel was located. The unsmiling officer pointed down a road to my right. Thanking them, I headed in that direction.

Ten minutes later as I approached the inn, which I realized was actually a bar and grill, I was startled by a figure that loomed out of the darkness and rain. It was another backpacker, who informed me that the four available bunks at the hostel were all taken but maybe I could sleep on the floor. That was the first hint that I was in for a bad night.

I thanked the hiker and walked over to what I assumed was the hostel. It was a cramped room, not much bigger than a walk-in closet. The small quarters were dirty, with the mud-covered gear of four hikers scattered around the room. The foul air and acrid smell of cigarettes hit my nostrils.

After one glance, I decided not to stay in that room, especially at ten dollars a night. There was a porch attached to the place, so I decided to ask the owner if I could sleep there for the night—which would keep me out of the rain and in the fresh air.

When I went into the adjacent bar to talk to the owner, I noticed right away that the place was animated. The Yankees and Angels game was playing on a loud TV over the bar. The place was crowded with men and women who were, to use a polite expression, socializing. I sat at the bar and ordered the large cheeseburger that was promoted on a sign outside, thinking that ordering would identify me as a paying customer. Besides, I was hungry.

While I waited for my cheeseburger, I talked to a gray-haired man on the stool next to me. He mentioned that his wife had died years ago, and I recognized him as one of the many lonely people who frequent bars just to have someone with whom to talk. Our conversation did not go very deep, but I was able to give a word of testimony and encourage the man to look to Christ for his spiritual needs. I don't normally patronize bars, but on my hike, a bar was often the only place I could find a meal; so I accepted the bar visits as an opportunity to talk with people I would never otherwise meet.

When the waitress arrived with my cheeseburger, I asked her about the possibility of sleeping on the hostel's porch that night. She went to check with the boss and returned to say that I could—for four dollars. I thought that was overpriced, but given that it was still raining, I didn't have much choice.

By moving some bags of cement around on the porch, I had just enough room to spread my ground cloth and sleeping bag. Tired after a long day of hiking, I was hoping for a good night's rest. It didn't happen.

First, I had been in my sleeping bag only a few minutes when a swarm of mosquitoes attacked. With one exception, they were worse than any I had encountered in the woods. I lathered on repellent and hunkered down in my bag, and after an hour the attacks diminished. *Finally,* I thought, *I will be able to sleep.*

But then, around midnight, a young woman emerged from the bar next to the hostel and got into a pickup truck. She started the motor, but before she could pull away, a man came out and began yelling insults at her. I was obliged to listen to the tirade taking place only ten yards from where I slept. Using obscene language, the man accused her of sleeping with his married friend. His language was so violent that I feared the verbal assault might be followed by a physical one.

This ugly exchange lasted for half-an-hour before the woman, obviously frightened, pulled away into the night, her tires screeching. I just had witnessed a scene from hell, a scene that I knew many people live all the time. As I prayed that the man and the woman would know the liberating power of Christ, I thanked God for saving me from such a life—which well could have been mine, had not Christ rescued me. That experience was also a reminder that Christians have been called to the dark places of the earth to bring the light of the gospel.

The next morning I was up at 6:00 A.M., groggy from lack of sleep. I found a general store, bought the food I needed, and returned to the trail.

I was nearing the end of my trek through New Jersey, and the New York State line wasn't far away. The seventy-three miles through the Garden State had been memorable, and I had been surprised and pleased by the amount of wilderness in New Jersey.

I had only one complaint about New Jersey, and it was a big one: although that part of the trail had fewer rocks, they were more difficult to navigate and more dangerous. The New Jersey rocks were so smooth and slippery when wet that at times it was like walking on ice. In my last day in New Jersey, I fell three times, suffering scrapes and bruises. The last time, I damaged one of my precious hiking poles, which, although badly bent, was fortunately still usable.

My first night on the New York AT was a bummer. I had hiked too late and got caught by the darkness. Again, my flashlight batteries gave out (too much reading at night), and I was unable to put up my tent. Thankfully, it wasn't raining and a few stars twinkled above. I spent that night sitting up, my back propped against a fallen tree and hoping no animals would be attracted to the food in my backpack. Huge planes from New York City flew over me, their lights blinking in the night sky. I imagined the plane's passengers sitting in their cushioned seats watching a movie, munching pretzels, and sipping Sprite, oblivious to the very uncomfortable hiker 20,000 feet below them.

I didn't sleep much that night, but eventually the dawn arrived and I continued hiking. In all, I slept out under the stars a half-dozen times on my 2,000-mile hike, and in God's good grace, I didn't get rained on once.

Bear Mountain Bridge was my destination for the day. I found a motel nearby, where I planned to catch up on the sleep I had lost the night before. After a long, hot shower I called Babs to get the latest news and was very happy to learn that I had received a letter from Skywalker, the trail maintainer who had asked Christ into his heart in Pennsylvania. He was rejoicing in his salvation and what God had done in his life. News that wasn't so encouraging, however, was that Hurricane Floyd had hit Florida with much destruction and was due to drop a lot of rain on New York in two or three days.

From Bear Mountain Bridge, West Point was just down the road. I would have enjoyed visiting the academy, but as usual, the trail was calling. That trail could be so demanding at times.

Walking across the Bear Mountain Bridge over the Hudson River was a pleasant experience. Four hundred years before, Henry Hudson and his crew had been astonished by the beauty of the region, and I felt the same admiration that day. Added to the beautiful view was the temperature change. It was a really hot day, but once I started hiking across the long bridge, it felt like someone had turned on a giant air conditioner. The cool breeze blowing across the bridge from the Hudson River was absolutely delightful.

One of my stops that week was at Graymore Manor. I'd been looking forward to staying at the Franciscan Friary at Graymore, but on arrival, I learned that hikers were now being lodged in an outdoor pavilion on the property. Although I would have enjoyed the experience of sleeping in a monastery, I was thankful for the pavilion. The only problem was the coyotes, which howled during the night from a nearby forest.

While hiking the next day, I stopped for a moment to talk with a man in his fifties who was hiking south. He said his trail name was Seiko. I already had noticed that his backpack, his clothing, his hair, and everything about him, looked perfectly in place. When I asked why he had chosen the name of an expensive watch, he said it was because he was striving for perfection.

I replied that there was only one person who was perfect—that was Christ, and He died for our sins. At that, Seiko erupted in anger and stalked off saying, "I've already heard enough about that." I had discovered long ago that people working for their salvation never find that the gospel is good news.

On September 14, I arrived at Dennytown campsite. It was a large facility, but that night, I was the only camper. I put up my tent, shaved (using only a cupful of water), and then ate supper. Feeling a bit lonely, I decided to build a fire, my first one on this section hike. Usually it's too late in the day, too wet, or I'm too tired to look for wood. But that night the conditions were just right.

Dead wood was scarce, but I found enough to make a small fire. The yellow flames leaped into the air and cheered my spirits. I've loved fires since I was a boy, when we lived for a year in a large house with a fireplace. I never have forgotten the flickering flames and the warmth. Whenever Babs and I went house hunting, I always tried to find one with a fireplace.

Sitting by the fire that night at Dennytown campsite, I felt an urge to sing some of my old scout songs. Although it had been fifty years since I was a scout, the words came back to me in almost perfect recall. With all the gusto I could muster, I sang my whole repertoire of songs, including some I had learned in French.

My singing turned to praises to God for all that He had done in my life. I saw that something as simple as joining a scout troop at age twelve was a preparation for the life God had planned for me. Satisfied, I reluctantly left the dying embers of my fire and crawled into my tent and fell asleep.

Chapter 18

Hit by
Hurricane Floyd

And there will be a tabernacle . . . for a place of refuge and
for a shelter from storms.

—Isaiah 4:6

Dennytown Campsite to Williamstown, Massachusetts

A ten-mile hike the next day brought me to a shelter known simply as RPH. The morning walk had been enjoyable as I passed through hemlock groves and inspiring views of surrounding lakes. In the afternoon, however, I walked in the rain. I wondered if this was the tail end of Hurricane Floyd.

Arriving at RPH Shelter, I found it to be an enclosed one-room structure with windows, a front door, and even a front porch. This was unusual, but I later recognized it as also providential. Two hikers were already at RPH, and their wet clothes were draped around the room. I decided that a third hiker's wet clothes, mine, would fill up the shelter uncomfortably.

About twenty yards from the RPH was a three-sided cinder block building, where I decided to stay for the night. The annex building worked out, except that during the heavy rains that night, the roof began to leak. Fortunately,none of the leaks were directly over my bunk, but I knew it was only a matter of time before they would reach me.

As I ate breakfast the next morning, Mud-Digger, one of the fellows who had stayed at RPH, stopped to talk with me. Despite the torrential rain, he was heading out on the trail. He was a good-looking, intelligent young man. We chatted for a few minutes, and since I had been reading in Romans that morning, I quoted Romans 6:23, "The wages of sin is death, but the gift of God is eternal life through Jesus Christ our Lord," and added a brief explanation.

I asked Mud-Digger what he thought about the verse I had just quoted. Did it make sense to him? He said that it did, and he was interested in spiritual things. In his pack he carried the book he was reading, *Mere Christianity* by C. S. Lewis. I told him that he had made a good choice and encouraged him in his spiritual quest. Then I shared with him what God had done in my life.

Finally he said that he had better get on the trail. Pulling the hood of his poncho over his head, he wished me luck on my hike and then walked out into the heavy rain. As I watched his tall figure disappear down the trail, I was again thankful for the great privilege of witnessing to some of the outstanding young people in America who hike the Appalachian Trail.

It was obvious that Hurricane Floyd had hit lower New York, and I decided then and there not to hike that day. Getting caught in a storm was one thing, but as far as I was concerned, starting out in one was folly. As a committee of one, I declared a day of rest for the Anderson Expedition. Day thirty-six would be my first non-hiking day.

RPH was now vacant, so I transferred my pack and gear to it and settled in, thankful for an enclosed building that protected me from the storm. The deluge continued, and before long, a small river was flowing past the front porch of the shelter. I was very glad that I had not ventured out on the trail that day. The intensity of the storm increased, and water cascaded off the shelter roof on all sides.

Above the clamor of the storm I worshiped God and sang His praises. Pacing the length of the small building, I thought of God's goodness to me throughout my life. While the storm raged, I had a blessed season of praise and intercession for family and friends. That I was on the AT to worship God was becoming increasingly clear to me, and one of my roles was to render to God the praise of which He alone is worthy. Thousands of hikers had walked the AT and gazed at all the beauty and magnificence, but how many had stopped to worship the One who created it all? Like a Trail Angel, I had been called by God to be a "Trail Choirboy," exalting Him there with my voice. I was enjoying my role with all my being.

My rest day also allowed me time to finish my paperback about D. L. Moody. The story of how God took an uneducated shoe salesman from Massachusetts and made him a great evangelist continued to inspire me.

By the next morning, Hurricane Floyd was spent. Big John, the shelter caretaker, took me into town to buy supplies. From the front seat of his van, I saw firsthand the devastation that Floyd had caused: roads were washed away and trees uprooted. John told me stories of hikers who had been caught in the storm and forced to flee to trail towns. Again, I silently thanked the Lord for providing the enclosed and relatively-comfortable refuge for me during the hurricane. Surely, that I had landed at RPH at just the right time was no accident. A faithful God had been watching over me.

I packed my fresh food supplies, swept out the shelter, and returned to the trail. The sun came out, and as I hiked along, I noted for the first time that fall was in the air. A certain something in the wind and in the woods announced that summer was over and autumn was upon us. I love this time of the year. *Bring it on,* I thought, reveling in all the nostalgic feelings that autumn carries.

Crossing the state line from New York to Connecticut on Day forty-two was a real boost to my confidence. My wagon was movin' on! That afternoon I took my lunch break at Indian Rocks and enjoyed the splendid view. Sitting on the ground with my back against a large rock, I could see for many miles and was perfectly content.

I just had finished my lunch when an older man and a younger man, probably father and son, arrived at the summit of Indian Rocks. They were day hikers and wore the Kippah caps that told me they were Jewish.

I remembered it was Yom Kippur weekend and wished them a happy holiday, which seemed to please them. Then I told them that I, too, was a child of Abraham through faith in Christ, who was a Jew. If they were shocked by my remark, it didn't register on their faces. I mentioned that I had been to Israel and how much I had enjoyed my visit. We talked for a few minutes, and when they left, I said, "Shalom."

Smiling, they returned the greeting. I hadn't been able to share the gospel with the two men, but I had identified myself as a Christian who was a friend of Israel, which I felt was important.

The weather was wet and miserable when I reached Kent, Connecticut, the next day. Somehow, hiking through those little, upscale New England towns made me feel grubbier than usual, and I was sure I looked quite miserable to the townsfolk. The contrast between their pristine cleanliness and my shabbiness was too stark for comfort. Evidently they were used to AT hikers because I encountered only one or two smartly-dressed people who seemed to look down their noses at me—and even that may have been my imagination.

I passed through a valley called Rand's View and was so taken with the beauty of that peaceful panorama that I stopped for lunch. However, my visit was cut short when I was attacked by swarms of small insects. I quickly closed my pack and moved on.

Eight miles later, I reached Riga Lean-to. (In Connecticut, a shelter is called a "lean-to.") Riga was not large, but it was relatively new and clean, and I was the lone occupant that night. By 8:00 everything was pitch-black, and then I was treated to a beautiful harvest moon. And I mean beautiful! With moonlight flooding the shelter, I sat in my sleeping bag gazing at the splendor until sleep overcame me. Someone said that an atheist's most embarrassing moment is when he is profoundly thankful for something in nature but doesn't know whom to thank. I didn't have that problem at Riga that night; I worshiped my Creator.

On September 25, I walked across the state line into Massachusetts, state number eleven on the AT. By now I had hiked 470 miles in this section, with only seventy more to go.

My first challenge was Sage Ravine. It was a little dangerous climbing down rocks into the ravine, but once I got there, it was pure delight to walk through the beautiful gorge, passing by its clear pools of water. I solemnly promised myself (as I did with a number of AT beauty spots) that someday I would return to Sage Ravine and hike it leisurely with my wife.

My second adventure in Massachusetts was climbing the rocky slope of Mount Everett. I remembered reading a hiker's humorous remark that this mountain was misnamed and should have been called "Mount Everest."

It was indeed a challenge, but an enjoyable one, and when I reached the summit, I was exuberant and aware of a change in my body. I was now a "lean, mean hiking machine." (By the end of this 500-plus mile section hike I would be twenty pounds lighter.) I had a hiker's legs and a hiker's lungs. And amazingly, I didn't dread climbing mountains anymore. Instead, I now looked forward to it. As so many hikers before me, I had learned to stop fighting the mountains and to "flow" with them. Actually, the change in my attitude surprised me more than the change in my physical condition.

On September 30, I found an inexpensive motel just off the trail several miles from Lee, Massachusetts. There I became acquainted with another hiker, Ron, who was in his forties and was also a section hiker. He hoped one day to do a thru-hike with his wife. Ron suggested we split the cost of a taxi fare to a restaurant in Lee. It was raining hard, and I readily agreed.

Our taxi driver took us to Joe's Diner. The name of the restaurant was certainly mundane, but its ambiance definitely was not. I wrote later in my journal:

> I was very impressed with Joe's Diner. The place was packed, and there was an air of friendly efficiency and excitement. The food (I got the pork dinner with mashed potatoes, gravy, and bread pudding) was mouth-watering and reasonably priced. I learned that Norman Rockwell had used the diner as the inspiration for one of his famous paintings: the one of the big policeman sitting at a restaurant counter staring down at the little boy next to him who was obviously running away.

My journal continued:

> On my hike I have been inspired by hardworking people who are innovative and who get the job done better than anyone else. People flock to these entrepreneurs. This is the spirit of America, one of its driving forces.

After our meal, while Ron and I waited on the street for our taxi back to the motel, I offered him a gospel tract. He refused it, saying,

"I have two brothers who are born again, and they've been trying to convert me for years."

I told Ron that I respected his desire not to discuss salvation, but I did an end-run, to use a football term—I gave him my personal testimony. I have learned over the years that even the most gospel-resistant person is curious about what God has done in someone else's life. Rarely will the unsaved refuse to listen to a testimony.

It was evident to me that the "Hound of Heaven" was on Ron's trail. Perhaps, even as we were talking, his brothers were praying for him. I was happy to be another link in the chain that might someday lead to his salvation.

It was raining the next morning when Ron waved good-bye to me. He headed south on the trail and I headed north. I stopped off in Dalton, Massachusetts, for a big breakfast of Belgian waffles, strawberries, and whipped cream. I noted in my journal that the last few days I had experienced hunger pangs that I couldn't seem to satisfy. But even though my stomach was feeling empty, my spirit was getting its fill with autumn beauty. The peak season was not yet upon Massachusetts, but the scenery was still beautiful to behold. I was seeing some reds and different shades of green, yellow, and brown. Added to that splendor were the abundant ferns along the trail. All in all, it was a feast for the eyes.

On October 3, I neared the end of my sixth AT section hike. My last night would be spent at Bascom Lodge, where I had reserved a bunk. To get to the lodge, I would have to hike up Mount Greylock, which meant climbing from 1,000 feet to 3,550 feet. On paper, that looked daunting; but to my surprise, it was a piece of cake. What took the strain out of the climb was the well-graded trail.

I arrived at the summit of Greylock in a thick fog. The nastiness of the weather outside was more than compensated for by the cozy comfort of Bascom Lodge, where a fire blazed in the fireplace and tea and cookies were laid out on a table next to comfortable couches and easy chairs. I relaxed in an over-stuffed chair and savored the warmth of the fire, thanking the Lord for His goodness.

A young couple with their two children sat near me, and we fell into conversation. When they learned that I had hiked to Massachusetts from the Maryland-Pennsylvania border, they were full of questions.

A hike of 530 miles boggled their minds, but I knew it was possible because of the Lord, who had given me the strength to take every step.

Bascom Lodge still was covered with fog the next morning when I departed. The trail down the north side of Mount Greylock was steeper and the rocks more slippery. I hiked slowly, not only because of the difficulty, but also because I wanted to meditate those last six miles and remember my experiences.

The first part of the morning was damp and overcast, but later a few rays of sun penetrated the gray. By the time I reached the road to Williamstown, where I would catch a bus to the airport, it was a crisp, sunny Sunday afternoon.

While hiking through Massachusetts, I had been surrounded by breathtaking views of the Berkshire Mountains. In 1907, a Presbyterian minister named Henry Van Dyke who visited the Berkshires was so inspired by the area that he wrote the jubilant hymn "Joyful, Joyful, We Adore Thee" to the music of Ludwig van Beethoven. I thought of the second stanza of that great hymn:

> All thy works with joy surround Thee,
> Earth and heaven reflect Thy rays,
> Stars and angels sing around Thee,
> Center of unbroken praise.
> Field and forest, vale and mountain,
> Flowery meadow, flashing sea,
> Chanting bird and flowing fountain,
> Call us to rejoice in Thee.

My heart rejoiced along with Henry Van Dyke in the Creator-God who made such a world, a world of nature that calls us to rejoice in Him. This was my great privilege in hiking the Appalachian Trail—to offer God the praise that He alone deserves. His glory was revealed with every step I took.

My AT guidebook suggested that when I reached the bottom of Mount Greylock, I turn around and look back. Heeding that advice, I turned and saw a spectacular portrait of fall beauty. That scene was a special reward from the Lord to encourage me as I ended my hike of 1999.

The Appalachian Trail

2000
150.6 miles hiked

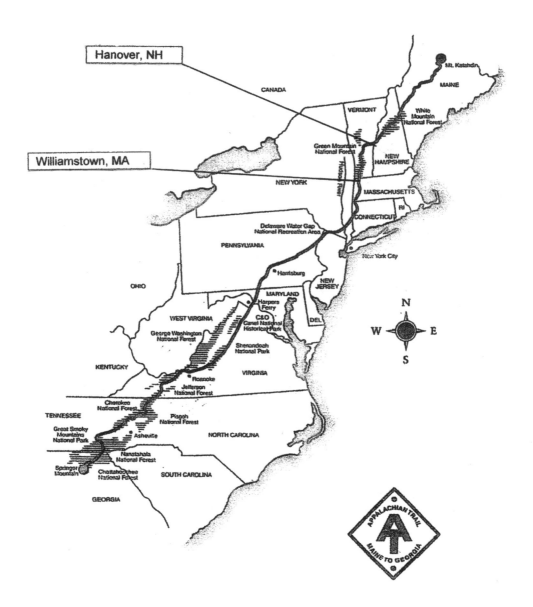

Chapter 19

"Are You Somebody Famous I Should Know?"

Under the shadow of the Almighty.

—Psalm 91:1

Williamstown, Massachusetts, to Hanover, New Hampshire

As I hiked deeper into New England, I moved deeper into my dreams. I'd grown up in northeastern Ohio and always enjoyed its maple trees, rural landscapes, and gentle hills, but New England was my first love. I had discovered that part of the US on a family vacation when I was fourteen, and that first enchantment with New England's charm never left me. When I married, I convinced my bride that the White Mountains would be the perfect place for our honeymoon, and the first week of our married life was immersed in the autumn splendor of New Hampshire.

I think that most northbound AT hikers have stars in their eyes as they move toward New England. Those states are a magnet pulling them irresistibly northward. New England would be the fabulous reward for all their sweat and suffering. Yes, the Great Smoky Mountains, Virginia, and Pennsylvania were all beautiful, but the splendor of New England would be the icing on the cake. And, despite their intimidation, the challenge of climbing its mountains only added to the excitement.

But before I left for my seventh AT section hike, I had an important date—with my wife. September 7, 2000, was the fortieth anniversary of our engagement. On a sunny morning forty years before, on a grassy knoll in Warren, Ohio's Packard Park, I had proposed to the girl of my dreams. She was sweet seventeen and we had to wait four years—while she completed Bible college and I began my missionary career in France—to marry. But that first acknowledgement of our love holds a special place in our memory.

Our anniversary celebration took place at a romantic bed and breakfast modeled after the book *Gone with the Wind* and appropriately named Tara. Although the price of our room and our ten-course dinner was way over our budget, it was worth every dime. That anniversary would encourage me many times in the next three weeks as I hiked through Vermont, even though at the time I didn't realize how much I would need that encouragement.

Early on September 9, my year-2000 hike was ready to roll. In total darkness, a small plane shuttled me from Youngstown, Ohio, to Pittsburgh, Pennsylvania, on the first leg of my journey to Massachusetts. When the flight attendant put my backpack in the hold, I discovered I was the only passenger on that flight. As the plane lifted into the sky, I chuckled to myself and wondered how many AT hikers had their own private plane.

In Boston I caught a bus to Williamstown, Massachusetts, the college town where I had ended my hike the year before. It felt good to be back in Williamstown. As I strolled through the town, I admired the stately campus of the 200-year-old college. However, I couldn't help wondering how far the college had drifted from the Christian principles of its founders.

Traveling by my thumb was usually not a problem for me, and it took me only a few minutes to hitch a ride back to the AT trailhead. Many years before, in my early twenties, I had hitchhiked from western Canada to Ohio, and I had spent exactly a dime on travel (when I took a bus across Calgary, Alberta). That had been a great adventure.

After thanking the driver for his kindness in giving me a ride, I hoisted my forty-pound pack and started hiking. Following the white blazes, I experienced the usual thrill of returning to the trail, but this time, the emotion seemed even stronger. In a sense, the AT had become my home. This was where I belonged, at least for the duration of my hike, and I was now back in my element.

After a few miles, I reached a black iron footbridge that crossed the Hoosic River. The sun was beginning to set as I stepped onto the bridge. At the far end, I noticed a man standing by the railing, gazing at the water. As I drew closer, I observed that he looked about fifty, had a weather-beaten face, and was wearing clothes that had seen better days.

The man greeted me, so I stopped to chat with him. I asked him what he was looking at. The man, Gary, was admiring a blue heron that he had spotted on a rock in the river. Blue herons are usually found along the ocean, not on rivers, so this may have added to the man's fascination.

I watched the bird with Gary for a moment and then asked him how things were going.

"Not well," he replied. "I fought in Vietnam and killed twenty-one of the enemy. I can't get that out of my mind."

We talked about war, God's love, and the peace that God gives when He comes into our lives.

Finally, I said that it was time for me to move on. I handed him a gospel tract and encouraged him to read it. Gary said he would and tucked the tract into his shirt pocket, right behind his pack of cigarettes.

I left the bridge and followed the trail, which climbed upward. When I reached the top of the hill, I heard someone calling and looked back. It was Gary, still standing on the iron bridge and waving his arms and shouting.

Stopping, I strained to hear what he was saying, and then caught his one-word message: "Peace."

I waved back, echoing his shout of peace, along with the prayer that Gary might find peace with God by the Holy Spirit opening his heart to Christ.

That night I pitched my tent in the woods at Sherman Brook campsite. There were platforms for tents, but because my tent was not freestanding, I had to stake it into the ground next to the platform. Feeling in a festive mood, I made a fire. The weather was mild, and a full moon was rising. I was happy with the several opportunities the Lord had given me that day to share the gospel. I sat alone by the fire and enjoyed an hour of prayer and fellowship with the Lord. By 8:00, when the last flames had died, I climbed into my tent and quickly fell fast asleep.

It took me only two miles of hiking the next morning to leave Massachusetts and walk over the state line into Vermont. Only three states remained between me and Mount Katahdin—and the end of a dream journey. But I knew that in those three states I would face the toughest challenges the AT had to offer. The White Mountains and the Presidential Range were waiting for me.

STRATTON MOUNTAIN

I had been looking forward to reaching Vermont's Stratton Mountain, which, in a sense, was the birthplace of the Appalachian Trail. According to legend, it was here that Benton McKaye, while he sat in a tree, had his vision of a continuous trail that would snake northward over the Appalachian mountains, from Georgia to Maine. In a good frame of mind, I walked down a charming spruce-lined trail to the hiker shelter. There is no official hiker refuge on Stratton Mountain, but hikers are permitted to stay in a ski-warming hut in off seasons.

Even though it was September, I was glad for an enclosed shelter that night. The wind was sharp, and a hint of winter chilled the mountain air. When I stepped into the wood-framed hut, I was greeted by a blast of warm air that wrapped itself around me like a cozy electric blanket on a cold night.

The hut was the size of a large living room, maybe twenty-five feet long and fifteen feet wide. Except for a small stove and a microwave in one corner, there were no furnishings. The heating system occupied a prominent place in another corner. The drone of its motor was loud, but I was not about to complain about the noise of the furnace because that's what produced the heat!

Several hikers already were settled in the warming hut, including, to my surprise, several children. This was the first time on my hike that I had come across children in a trail shelter. A muscular man of about forty, with his black hair in a ponytail, introduced himself as the father and a younger woman sitting nearby as the children's mother.

I learned that this family of five was thru-hiking the AT from Maine to Georgia, and I was amazed at what they already had accomplished. They had hiked through the Maine wilderness and over the Presidential Mountains. The three children included a fourteen-year-old son; a daughter of about twelve; and their youngest, a little girl aged two, who "hiked" on her father's back in a special hiking harness. I smiled at the trail name of this cute little blonde: Easy Rider.

I agreed wholeheartedly with the father that the hike was a fantastic learning experience for the kids. They would mature much faster than in a classroom. This family had my admiration for even attempting such an ambitious (and potentially dangerous) venture. Knowing how hard at times it was to organize myself, the logistics of organizing a family expedition of this kind boggled my mind. I wished them well. A year later, I was happy to read in an AT journal that their adventure had been successful; they had reached Springer Mountain in Georgia, the southern terminus of the AT.

By 9:00 that evening, things had quieted down. We all, kids included, were in our sleeping bags on the floor of the warming hut. Space was at a minimum, but I'd found a niche between the wall and the heating system just big enough for me and my sleeping bag. I was dozing off when the door banged open, and in walked two more hikers.

I opened my eyes just wide enough to see two young men in their late teens. Then I noticed something strange: one of them was wearing what looked like the bottom half of a frilly woman's dress. *What in the world?* I thought. But it was late, and I was too groggy to deal with strange hiking attire. I closed my eyes and went to sleep.

The next morning I found the two late arrivals parked almost in front of me, which was the only space left. As we prepared our breakfast in the cramped quarters, the two hikers and I exchanged trail names and chatted about conditions on the trail. As we talked, my foggy guess of the night before was confirmed: the two young men were gay. To my knowledge, this was the first time I had encountered homosexuals on the trail. Evidently, the frilly dress was their way of making a statement.

As a Christian, I take seriously what the Bible says about homosexuality, and my spirit was grieved that these two fellows had bought into a destructive lifestyle. I prayed that I might have opportunity to witness to them.

The opportunity came later that morning, when rounding a bend on the trail I saw the two fellows sitting on a log, taking a break. Believing this moment as an answer to my prayer, I greeted them again and spent a few minutes chatting with them. Then I offered them a gospel tract, explaining briefly its message and adding my own testimony of what Christ had done for me. The men listened but made no comment. Finally, wishing them a good hiking day, I moved down the trail, happy for the privilege of sharing with these two young fellows the greatest story ever told.

A Narrow Escape

Manchester Center, Vermont, was my next destination, and I covered the fourteen miles from Stratton Mountain to Manchester Center in good time. Even thumbing a ride from the trail into town was no problem. It was all so easy and pleasant that as I walked down the main street, I could not have guessed that this quaint little New England town would be the scene of one of the most dangerous moments of my entire AT hike.

My first stop in Manchester Center was at Friendly's® restaurant for fried chicken and a chocolate milkshake that was so huge I couldn't finish it. Being served a shake that was larger than my appetite was a rare experience on the trail. Considering myself something of a connoisseur, on my way out, I complimented the woman at the checkout counter on their milkshakes.

I then walked up a hill to the hiker hostel listed in my trail guide. The hostel, actually a home, was comfortable, and the owner was friendly. However, he had one restriction: because he spent many hours on the Internet for his business, hikers could not talk on the phone for more than one minute. When I explained I would need at least ten minutes to talk with my wife, he said that there was a public phone just a couple of blocks away.

Once I settled in my room, I took a hot shower and then watched the evening news. With my spirits revived, I decided to walk to the public phone and call my wife. By then it was almost dark, and I had trouble locating the phones. But after asking directions from a pass-erby, I found them. I got through to Babs easily, but noise from passing cars made conversation difficult. We had a brief but helpful exchange of news and updates. Before hanging up, I assured her of my love, and then said "good-bye," not knowing at the time they could have been our last good-byes.

After hanging up, I glanced at my watch: 10:20 p.m. and almost completely dark. As I stepped out to the curb and began to cross the street, I saw the headlights of a car heading towards me. I felt no particular concern because I was on a crosswalk and the approaching car seemed not to be traveling very fast. But by the time I reached the middle of the street, my panic button turned on. The car was moving faster than I realized and gave no indication of slowing down. Adrenalin took over, and I sprinted to the opposite curb. I thought I had reached safety, when I felt the sickening thud of impact—the car had smashed into my left leg.

I went down on the side of the road. The impact made such a noise that people at a nearby convenience store came running out to see what happened. Although in shock, I managed to get to my feet and hobble over to the store, where someone brought out a chair. I collapsed into it.

Someone else called 911, and I was told an ambulance was on its way. The police arrived before the ambulance and questioned me to determine my degree of shock: What day was it? What was my name? Where was I from? I was shaken up, but I think most of my answers were right.

At first, it looked like it was going to be a hit-and-run, but then the driver of the car, a badly shaken woman in her sixties, had returned to the scene of the accident and now stood at the edge of the small crowd. She claimed she hadn't seen me, that I had come out of nowhere. There might have been some mitigating factors because of the darkness, but my being on the crosswalk established clearly that I was in the right.

The ambulance arrived, and I was put on a stretcher and whisked away to a hospital in Dalton, Vermont, thirty miles away. During the trip, a medical assistant continued a stream of questions in an effort to keep me conscious. When I expressed my gratitude to God that I was still alive, the questions stopped.

At the hospital, my leg was x-rayed to determine the extent of my injuries. Then a young doctor came to the examining room to give me the results. When he learned that I had been hiking the Appalachian Trail, he jokingly said, "Are you someone famous that I should know?" I assured him that I was not.

My greatest fear was that I would not be able to return to the trail, or worse, that I would never hike again. I was greatly relieved when the doctor told me that I had no broken bones. Given the force of the impact, I considered that a small miracle. He said I did have a very deep bruise on my calf and that I would need to stay off my feet for a couple of days.

Upon reflection later, I realized that what had spared me more serious injury was that my leg was in mid-air when it was hit and had given with the direction of the impact. In addition, my high-top hiking boots had given me a measure of protection. Had the car hit my right leg, which was on the ground, I would have been in real trouble. Beyond that, I knew, it was God's mercy. I estimated that the woman's car was traveling about forty miles an hour, and had I been a step behind, I probably would have become another traffic fatality.

The hospital called a taxi to return me to the hiker hostel in Manchester, and I made the journey in the front seat of the cab with my left leg propped up on the dashboard on a bag of ice. During the thirty-minute ride back to Manchester, I had an excellent opportunity to talk to Ray, the cab driver, about spiritual matters. Recently divorced, Ray was moonlighting as a cabbie. He was still hurting from his divorce but seemed open to the gospel and my testimony. I felt our half-hour together was definitely another "God appointment." If nothing else, my accident had ushered me into the life of a spiritually-needy cabdriver.

It was nearly 1:00 A.M. when I returned to the hostel. Fortunately, the door was unlocked. (Bless the small-town sense of security!) With difficulty, I climbed the stairs to my room and removed my clothes.

After swallowing a couple of pain pills, I went to bed with the ever-present ice pack under my leg. As I lay there reflecting on the events of the previous twenty-four hours and the opportunities God had given me to witness, another thought occurred to me. *Could there be a connection between my witnessing and the accident?* By telling hikers and others about Christ, I was invading enemy territory, and I couldn't help wondering if my mission had put me on Satan's hit list. That he was trying to silence my witness on the trail could be only speculation on my part, but it did give me food for thought and a new appreciation for the protection of God's ministering angels.

Manchester Center was not far from Rutland, Vermont, where good friends Paul and Ruthie Meigs lived. Paul and I went way back to high school days in Ohio, and we had been in each other's weddings. They had moved to Vermont many years ago. Remembering the doctor's orders to rest a few days, I called Paul and asked him if he and Ruthie would like a houseguest for the weekend. They graciously agreed, and an hour later, Paul, smiling as usual, pulled up in front of the hostel to take me to their home in the country.

I had a refreshing off-the-trail weekend. Not only was I treated to Ruthie's fabulous home cooking, but also on Sunday morning, I was asked to give a brief report on the work in France at the Baptist church they attend. Standing behind a pulpit dressed in hiking clothes and sporting a bandaged leg was an unusual experience for me. But the folks were gracious, and by now I was used to being out of step with the civilized world.

Paul shuttled me back to the trail on Monday, September 21, and then hiked an hour with me. The warm fellowship the Meigs extended to me that weekend cheered my heart and helped me to recover from the trauma of being hit by a car. Their kindness was one of the thousand blessings God gave me during my hike. I had to hike now with a noticeable limp, but at least I was still hiking.

Vermont dazzled me with its splendor. The Green Mountains were a paradise of natural beauty and outstanding landscape, and the climb up Killington Peak was awesome. I voted Vermont the most stunning state on the trail, up to that point. Knowing I would see spectacular sights farther north, I reserved my final judgment until the end. But I never would forget the magnificent scenery that I was privileged to hike through in Vermont.

My original plan for this section was to hike to Crawford Notch in New Hampshire, a total of 220 miles. However, because my leg was not completely healed and I was still feeling some pain and favoring that leg in difficult terrain, I reluctantly concluded that I should terminate my hike for that year in Hanover, New Hampshire. I just didn't feel that my bruised leg was ready for the difficult climbs I would face in the White Mountains.

I was disappointed that I would hike only 150 miles in 2000, but given the situation, I was fortunate to have hiked that far. The Lord had been gracious. In Hanover, I called Babs and found that she had faithfully researched all the information I needed for my flight from Hanover to Ohio. What a wife! Who needed a travel agent?

As my plane lifted off from Hanover the following morning, I was already planning my last section hike for 2001. Katahdin was now in my sights. I still had 441.5 miles left to cover, but I knew that with the Lord's help, I could make it. I was already savoring the taste of victory.

The Appalachian Trail

2001
441.5 miles hiked

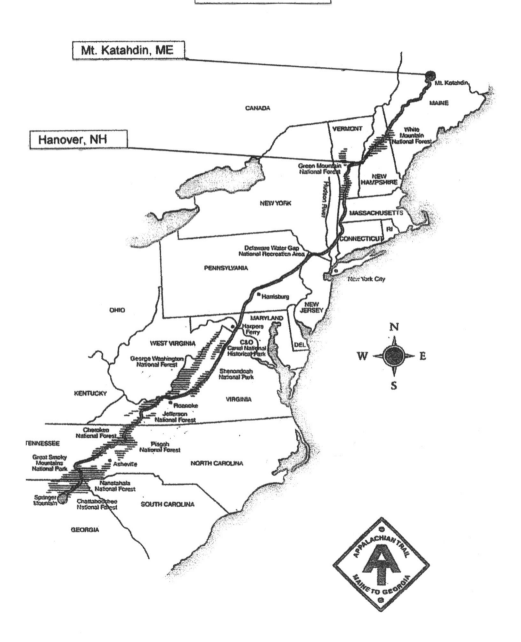

Mt. Katahdin, ME

Hanover, NH

Chapter 20

My Toughest Day
on the Trail

I will make the wilderness a pool of water.

—Isaiah 41:18

Hanover, New Hampshire,
to South Jacob's Brook

It was raining hard the early morning of August 3, 2001, when long-time friend Arden Hull drove me the seven miles from our home to Youngstown Airport in Ohio. I was flying to New Hampshire to begin my final section hike on the AT. This last hike of 441.5 miles would take me to the summit of Mount Katahdin, where I would finish the experience of a lifetime.

Perhaps sensing that this trip was special, Arden, a deacon in our church, sat with me in the airport, chatting about my hike, church, and other matters. We had known each other fifty years, attending the same church, so conversation came easily. After half an hour, Arden left, assuring me that he and the church would be praying for me. Certain that I would need those prayers, I was grateful for them. An hour later, I was on my flight to Pittsburgh, where I would catch another flight to Boston.

In Pittsburgh, I boarded my plane for Boston, but after it had taxied to the runway, we learned there would be a delay. During the wait, I talked with my seatmate, a thirty-five-year-old man of Irish descent from Boston. As it turned out, we had several mutual interests. We had both run the Boston Marathon. He wanted to hike the Appalachian Trail. And he had spent time in France. Those subjects provided us with a half-hour of interesting conversation.

Though I detected no special interest in spiritual matters in my new friend, he listened well as I shared the gospel with him. He didn't hesitate in accepting the tract I offered him, "How to Seek God." I knew that while I was talking to this man, the Holy Spirit was speaking to him with words far beyond my feeble explanations. And I was sure that the Lord had ordered the delay of our takeoff and the resulting conversation.

Until now, getting to the starting point of each section hike had been relatively easy, but on this trip, I had plenty of problems. After arriving in Boston too late for my flight to Lebanon, New Hampshire, I was told that the flight had been canceled and that we passengers would be driven to our destination.

I found myself in a van with five others and the driver. Shortly after leaving Boston, we were hit by a fierce rainstorm that was accompanied by deafening thunder and lightning strikes all around us. The roads became clogged with traffic, and our progress was very slow. Not surprisingly, our driver and my fellow passengers were showing signs of emotional stress. I felt a bit like the Apostle Paul on the ship engulfed by a storm on his way to Rome to preach the gospel.

Eventually the storm subsided, and we reached the airport at Lebanon, near Hanover. But then I discovered that my backpack had not arrived from Boston. I had with me only my wallet and the clothes on my back and no place to stay for the night.

I called around to motels and discovered that, because of a Shriners' convention and a high school football game, everything was booked. After trying repeatedly, I finally located a room at a Best Western, but at an exorbitant price. I considered spending the night at the airport, but it was so small and uncomfortable that I gave up on that idea.

I took the room at Best Western, and a cab delivered me there. Once in my room, I had no toilet articles, no pajamas—nothing. I did find a Gideon Bible in a drawer (bless the Gideons!) and read several chapters in Colossians to comfort my soul. With all the problems I was encountering, discouragement was knocking at my door.

I did not sleep well and was up early the next morning. After a continental breakfast and a conversation with a Tennessee bus driver who was interested in spiritual things, I caught a cab back to the airport and was very happy to learn that my backpack had arrived. But my trekking poles had not made the trip!

I went to the baggage claim office and told the staff that I could not hike without my poles. They were sympathetic and assured me that something would be done. Within half an hour, a young man named Roland presented himself and said that because the trekking poles could not be located, the airline would purchase me new ones. That was welcome news.

Roland then took me to a large sporting goods store, where it took me only five minutes to pick up a pair of Leki hiking poles for $130, paid for by the airline. That was at least some consolation after all the time and money I had lost. I also had an excellent conversation with Roland.

This had turned out to be the toughest start of any of my hikes. And the problems were not over. In fact, my greatest trial lay directly ahead of me. Roland let me off, along with my backpack and new trekking poles, at noon, in the middle of a Shriners' parade in Hanover. So much for the quiet visit to Dartmouth College campus that I had planned!

Hanover that day was the scene of street noise and loud music, with drums and blaring trumpets. I turned down a quiet side street and found a restaurant specializing in pizza. Knowing I would soon be back in the wilderness, I ate huge slices of pepperoni pizza, putting what was left in my pack for the next day. I then tried to call Babs to let her know how things were going but couldn't get through to her.

It was 2:30 by the time I left Hanover and began my last section hike on the AT. I was happy to be back in the wilderness and wondered what adventures awaited me in the 441.5 miles that lay between Hanover and the summit of Mount Katahdin.

One of the first things I noticed on the trail was a scarcity of water. Having never hiked this early in August, I hadn't been exposed to really severe drought on the AT. There were a few times in Virginia and Pennsylvania when water had been hard to come by, but rangers and trail angels had left plastic jugs of water near crossroads on the trail. In New Hampshire, I found neither rangers nor angels. On days one and two, I was able to coax a little water from the springs for my bottles. But by day three, I was finding that instead of springs, there were mud holes.

I was feeling weaker and weaker as I climbed Smarts Mountain. As I expected, the spring on Smarts also was dried up. My two quarts of water had been used up long ago, and I was becoming desperate. An elderly hiker I met heading south gave me a half-cup of water, but I felt guilty accepting it from his small reserve. Besides, my body was now so dehydrated that what I needed was not a half-cup of water; I needed half-a-gallon.

Increasingly, I was feeling the effects of my extreme thirst. My thinking was disoriented, and my body was shutting down. I searched through my pack for something, anything, liquid that I could drink. All I came up with was a small bottle of mouthwash, which I gulped down. But that only made matters worse; the alcohol hitting my stomach just increased my disorientation. I was close to going into shock.

I had begun to experience some of the symptoms described by historian Nathaniel Philbrick in his book *In the Heart of the Sea* (Penguin Putnam Inc., New York, 2000). He recounted the experiences of Pablo Valencia, a forty-year-old sailor-turned-prospector, who survived almost seven days in the Arizona desert without water:

> Saliva becomes thick and foul-tasking; the tongue clings irritatingly to the teeth and the roof of the mouth . . . A lump seems to form in the throat . . . severe pain is felt in the head and neck. The face feels full due to shrinking of the skin. Hearing is affected, and many people begin to hallucinate. Then comes the agonies of a mouth that has ceased to generate saliva.

My Toughest Day on the Trail

I looked at my map and saw that five miles down the trail was a stream named South Jacob's Brook. But five miles is a long way when you're dangerously dehydrated, and there was no guarantee that the brook would not be dried up like the springs. I had no choice but to press on and pray that there would be water at the brook. Fortunately, the trail was downhill. I would not have had the strength to hike uphill.

I started towards the brook. Then I realized after two miles that I was too weak to make it with the weight of my pack. So I hid my pack in the woods and continued on without it, carrying just two empty plastic water containers and a drinking cup.

To say I walked to the brook would be an exaggeration. I *staggered* toward it, at times feeling like I would fall over, and all the time crying to the Lord to help me in my distress. I was dizzy and had trouble focusing on the trail.

Just before I reached South Jacob's Brook, I heard the most beautiful sound in the world—the noise of water flowing, bubbling over rocks! I could smell the water! With my last ounce of strength, I reached the embankment above the brook and rolled down the fifteen feet to the water's edge.

I could hardly move because as I came down the mountain my legs started cramping, "locking up." Lying prostrate on the ground, I dipped my cup into the brook, which was actually a rushing mountain stream, and began drinking—and drinking, and drinking for almost thirty minutes. It took that long for my body to become hydrated.

This was the first time in my life I had come that close to dying of thirst, but gradually my strength returned. I filled my water bottles and walked slowly back up the mountain to retrieve my pack from where I had hidden it. Turning around, I retraced the five miles down the mountain, past the brook, and to a campsite. What a day!

That evening I read Psalm 121, noting especially the words, "He will not let thy foot slip . . . He will keep thee from harm" (KJV). Those words from the Lord were in my mind as I crawled into my tent and fell into an exhausted sleep.

Chapter 21

Mount Lafayette—
Almost Heaven

They saw no one any more, but only Jesus with themselves.
—Mark 9:8

South Jacob's Brook to Mount Lafayette

GLENCLIFF AND DENNIS

After the stress of my first week on the trail in New Hampshire, I felt the need for some R & R. That need was met when I arrived at a village with the quaint name of Glencliff, New Hampshire. This little community is home to a hostel run by three men in their forties named Packrat, Big John, and Moonbow. I was impressed by the relaxed yet sincere and organized effort of these men to meet the needs of long-distance hikers. They are a part of the small army of wonderful people who make the AT experience possible.

The Glencliff hostel was the perfect place for me to recover my strength and prepare for the serious challenges of the White Mountains. I found a place on the upper floor of a barn that had been turned into a dormitory. One side of the barn was open to the wilderness, which added to its attractiveness. To keep hikers comfortable in the

August heat and humidity, a large fan had been installed in the upper loft. My first act at Glencliff was to stretch out on my sleeping bag and pad in the afternoon and sleep for an hour.

That evening, I went to a nearby restaurant with several other hikers for fried chicken, pizza, two Barq's® root beers, one Pepsi®, and a quart of chocolate milk. I was in hiker heaven! I could eat all those goodies and not worry about putting on weight because I would burn up the calories on the trail. My overindulgence came with a price, however, because I didn't sleep well that night.

One of the hikers staying in the barn was a thirty-year-old named Dennis. Because I thought his trail name, Maniac, didn't flatter him, I chose to call him by his real name. It often puzzled me that a surprising number of hikers chose trail names that were unflattering. Things could be discouraging enough on the trail without the burden of a negative name. But, perhaps it was some people's way of lowering expectations for themselves. My trail name, "Onward," constantly encouraged me to press toward the goal I had set.

Dennis was a lanky, friendly guy from Atlanta, Georgia, who spoke with a soft, Jimmy Carter accent. He was divorced and had a young son. Dennis was a locksmith by trade, and from the description he gave of his work, I had the impression that he was good at it. His employer had given him six months off to hike the AT, and like me, he was heading for Katahdin.

Dennis seemed to enjoy talking about God and the Bible, which I appreciated, but I wasn't sure where he stood in terms of a personal faith in Christ. In general, though, we hit it off well, and he seemed happy to spend time with me. Dennis did have a vice: he would stop every hour on the hour to smoke. To me, cigarette smoke and pristine wilderness did not go together, but I made a charitable effort to overlook his weakness.

Dennis and I hiked Mount Moosilauk together. Because this was considered a tough mountain to climb, we decided to slack-pack (a term coined by backpackers) by leaving our heavy backpacks at Glencliff and hiking with relatively light daypacks. This was a wise decision because the trail was very rocky. One portion of the trail went near a huge cascade, and though iron railings had been installed to help hikers keep their footing on the smooth, slippery rocks, hiking was still precarious. The entire climb was difficult, even with daypacks. A shuttle picked us up at the end of the day and returned us to the hostel.

Another hiker I met at Glencliff was a man with a biblical trail name, Jabaz. He was a Christian and carried Bibles in his pack to distribute to other hikers. I had to admire this brother's zeal, as even three or four Bibles can add a lot of weight to a pack.

After Glencliff and the Moosilauk climb, Dennis and I stayed at a hiker hostel in North Woodstock, an attractive tourist town, but whose main street looked to a wilderness hiker like Las Vegas. It was raining, and the hostel in North Woodstock was full. The owner said we could sleep on the porch for eight dollars. That seemed a bit overpriced, but the rain limited our options. That evening, we had a fabulous meal at the Truant Restaurant, a favorite hangout for hikers. The barbecued ribs were savory and the company congenial.

As we hiked, I would often share truth from Scripture with Dennis. He never refused my mini-sermons. After our night on the porch of the hostel, we had breakfast at Peg's Restaurant. Following the meal, I took out my Bible and read a psalm to Dennis. His reaction caught me off guard; when I finished, he snatched the Bible from my hand and ran over to a hiker seated at a nearby table and said, "Listen to this!" Dennis proceeded to read the same passage to the startled hiker. I sat bemused as I witnessed the spread of God's Word in unexpected ways.

Two days later, I faced another challenge: the 4,400-foot Mount Kinsman. By now Dennis was hiking ahead of me. My pace was slowing down in the White Mountains. I noted in my journal that the climb up South Kinsman Mountain was "one of my hardest days on the trail. I just inched up the mountain, hand over hand."

On the map, the 5,000-foot Mount Lafayette looked like one tough escalade. But, perhaps because it was well graded, I didn't find the climb all that difficult. In fact, I enjoyed it. When I reached the summit, I fell in love with Mount Lafayette. To this day, I remember that particular climb and summit as my Appalachian Trail "mountaintop experience."

The weather on August 15, 2001, was perfect as I climbed Lafayette. The sky was clear as the finest crystal. I knew that days like this are uncommon in "the Whites," and thus special. I wrote in my journal, "What can I say to describe the beauty of Lafayette? It's just out of this world."

I arrived at the summit of Mount Lafayette at 7:00 in the evening. Dennis was already there, along with a half-dozen other young hikers. When he saw me climbing the last two hundred yards towards the mountain's summit, he ran down to where I was, took my pack, and carried it up to the top of the mountain. I was touched by his thoughtfulness. As we climbed those last one hundred yards together, I sang the hymn "How Great Thou Art." Dennis listened, and when I finished he said, "Man, I really like that song."

On the summit of Lafayette I noticed the ruins of what had been a large stone building and learned that they were the remains of a hotel that had stood there a century ago. Because the stone blocks offered some protection from the forceful winds, the young hikers planned to spend the night there. I decided to join them and found a spot where the two-foot high stones partially broke the wind. I spread out my pad and sleeping bag.

A mile below us we could see Greenleaf Hut, the hiker lodge where we could have spent the night. I think that all of us sensed that this evening was a very special moment in our experience. Perhaps never again would we have the privilege of being in this incredible place in such perfect weather. Looking back, I would not have traded my night on Mount Lafayette for a room at Buckingham Palace.

I was finishing my supper when I sensed a movement in the group, as if something dramatic was about to take place. Several hikers had grabbed their cameras and were heading to a point more exposed than our stone block refuge. I grabbed my camera and followed them.

We found ourselves on a large, rocky plateau that looked out on a magnificent range of mountains that presented unbelievable splendor. But our attention was focused on something else—the setting sun. Stunned by the breathtaking beauty unfolding before our eyes, no one spoke a word. No shutters clicked, no one moved. We were eyewitnesses to God's majesty. A holy hush had settled on our small group as we sensed His awesome power and presence.

I stood on Lafayette's rocky plateau meditating and worshipping God at 5,000 feet. Later I wrote in my journal, "I don't expect ever again to witness such majestic beauty."

We returned to the ruins and snuggled into goose-down sleeping bags. It promised to be a very cold night, and zipping the hood of my sleeping bag as tightly as I could around my face, I breathed a prayer of thanksgiving to God for an incredible experience. As I drifted off to sleep in that pristine mountain air, an unpleasant odor reached my nostrils. Somewhere out in the darkness, Dennis was smoking his last cigarette of the day—a forceful reminder that I was not yet in heaven, and the best still lay ahead.

Chapter 22

"I Survived the World's Worst Weather."

Blessed be the Lord who daily loads us with benefits.
—Psalm 68:19

Mount Lafayette to Mount Washington

I was now in the heart of the Presidential Range, and its most famous mountain, Mount Washington, was just ahead. I was excited. There would be tough climbing, but with God's help, I already had conquered several impressive mountains and lived to tell the story. I wasn't breaking any speed records, and younger hikers passed me on a regular basis. I kept up my slow, steady pace and sometimes caught up with them. The sixty-seven-year-old turtle at times passed the hare.

One of the distinctive features of the White Mountains is the hut system. The huts, an important part of the Whites' romantic history, are rustic lodges, some of them dating back to the 1930s. They are all constructed similarly, each with a large dining hall and adjacent rooms that hold a large number of bunk beds.

Each hut is staffed by a crew of mostly young people who prepare the meals and take care of other needs. There is no effort to make things fancy, but just to tend to the basic needs of trail hikers. I had been told that long-distance hikers could earn a free meal and a night's lodging by serving tables.

The first hut that I came across was Galehead. I probably could have dug up the money to pay for a night at Galehead, but I decided that working at a hut would be an interesting part of my trail experience. Forty years earlier I had served tables and washed dishes in college, so I had some experience.

I asked the thirtyish woman in charge at Galehead if I could work in exchange for lodging and food. She looked a little surprised at my request, but said "yes." I learned that night that "lodging" did not involve a bed; it was the privilege of sleeping on one of the tables! But at least I was under a roof, and the food was good and plentiful.

My work consisted of wiping off tables, setting them, serving food, and sweeping floors. Being a busboy was humbling. I asked the Lord to give me a servant's heart and make me more like Him through the experience.

Getting to know crew members and talking to hikers helped me better understand the hut system. A lot of families had come to the huts wanting a taste of hiking in the Whites without the difficulties of backpacking. The hut system facilitated that admirable desire. It was a fine family experience.

I left Galehead after breakfast the next morning and continued hiking at my slow pace. Clearly, speed was not the name of the game in the White Mountains because hiking was slow and difficult. I was lucky if I could grind out seven miles a day.

Two days later, I arrived in Crawford Notch, and from there I hitched a ride to a hostel on Route 302, where I reserved a bunk for the night.

After locating my bunk and settling in, I looked around the area and was delighted to discover that within a stone's throw of the hostel was a trail leading up Mount Willard. As mountains go, Willard is neither impressive nor well-known, and it's not very high. However, its summit offers a panoramic view of Crawford Notch. And for me, Willard held another, special attraction. Babs and I had climbed that mountain thirty-seven years before on our honeymoon and had tackled the challenge with all the enthusiasm of young lovers.

With amusement, I remembered that we were tired after only forty-five minutes of our climb. We stopped to rest, and an elderly couple passed us on their way down the mountain. When they were out of earshot, Babs and I laughed at our weariness compared to the vigor of that elderly couple.

A few minutes later, we reached the summit of Mount Willard and were thrilled with the inspiring view of Crawford Notch. Hand in hand, my bride and I looked at the expanse before us and thought of the life voyage on which we were embarking. The future was bright and beautiful.

Now, looking at the trail up Mount Willard, I would have loved to climb it again, but I didn't have the time—I had laundry to do!

LAUNDROMAT FELLOWSHIP

From the hostel I hitched a ride to a nearby community, where I'd heard there was a Laundromat. Trail town Laundromats were one of my favorite places—they were always warm and sweet smelling—and once inside the Laundromat, I appreciated its warmth. Even in late August the air of the White Mountains was crisp, hinting that autumn was just around the corner.

I threw my dirty hiking clothes into the washer and then into the dryer. By now I knew the drill by heart, and I was folding my dry clothes and putting them into a clean plastic bag when a couple in their fifties came into the Laundromat. They introduced themselves as Dennis and Cathy Evangelos from Massachusetts.

As we talked about the weather, I had what Christians call the "witness of the Spirit" and felt sure these folks were believers. That proved later to be true.

Although we had just met, we talked like old friends. Quiet Dennis was a pipefitter, and outgoing Cathy was passionate about the Appalachian Trail. She was full of questions about my hike. Cathy was typical of millions of Americans who probably never will step foot on the AT but who, nevertheless, are fascinated by the trail and want to learn all they can about it. I considered it my privilege not only to hike the AT, but also to share my adventures with AT enthusiasts so that they could experience some of the thrills vicariously.

The Evangeloses invited me to supper that evening, an invitation I said I gladly would accept after I had showered and shaved. They took me back to the hiker hostel in Crawford Notch and returned an hour later to take me to supper at a restaurant they knew.

That evening, over delicious barbecue ribs and scallops, we discussed our families, what God had been doing in our lives, and of course, my experiences on the AT. We spent a pleasant evening together, and when we separated, we exchanged addresses and promised to keep in touch. Crawling into my bunk at the hostel that night, my heart overflowed because all the things that were happening to me were a part of God's wonderful plan.

THE CROWN JEWEL

I returned to the trail and began climbing Mount Washington, the crown jewel of the White Mountains. My first stop was Lake of the Clouds Hut, where I planned to spend the night. Great was my delight when upon my arrival at the Hut I was able to purchase a large bowl of piping-hot vegetable soup for $2.00. However, to my chagrin, I later learned that the bowl was "bottomless" and I could have had several more servings. There was a spiritual lesson in that little incident. Many Christians fail to recognize that God's grace is boundless ("bottomless"), and they content themselves with much less than God wants to give them. They take only one bowl of His grace when they could have many.

Like the other huts, the cost for lodging and food was pretty steep, more than I wanted to pay. I could have worked cleaning and serving tables again, but I would have lost time. My plans were to get an early start the next morning on my way to the summit of Mount Washington.

Another option was "The Dungeon," a room I had read about in books by AT hikers who had spent a night at Lake of the Clouds. I decided to give it a try. I approached the young man in charge of lodging at Lake of the Clouds and asked, "Is there room in the Dungeon?"

He replied positively but with a negative look on his face. I discovered why when I located the Dungeon; it looked like something from Dante's *Inferno*. Situated underneath the building, it held five bunks—three on one side of the wall, two on the other—with everything crammed into that small, damp, cave-like room. A hiker with even a hint of claustrophobia would have fled the place.

But the charge for a night in the Dungeon was only $6.00. I was so exhausted that I flopped down on the middle bunk on the left wall and promptly fell into a stupor that lasted an hour. When I awoke, it was only four in the afternoon, but I felt absolutely drugged. That was a blessing in disguise, though, because I was much less aware of my miserable surroundings.

Later, four other hikers, including a couple from Iowa, joined me in the Dungeon. I had an interesting conversation with the couple from Iowa, and one of the other hikers gave me two candy bars to lighten his pack. So, it wasn't all bad. And knowing I had the experience of sleeping in the fabled hole-in-the-wall that had been the resting place for many famous AT hikers over the decades improved my attitude.

The next morning I was out of the Dungeon by 6:30 and on my way to the summit of Mount Washington. According to the map, I was only 1.6 miles from the top. As predicted, the weather was bad.

I had been on the trail only a few minutes when I ran into fog that grew thicker with every step I took. By the time I reached the summit, I was in the thickest pea soup fog that I ever had encountered. I could barely see beyond the end of my nose—and my nose is not especially long.

At the summit, I needed to locate the Sherman Adams Summit building, so I wandered around in the fog, hoping to bump into the building and feeling much like the proverbial blind man in a dark room chasing a black cat that isn't there.

Just as my panic alarm was about to go off, I stumbled onto the Adams building. Breathing a prayer of thanks, I entered the main entrance and immediately was shocked. The dated wooden structure that my bride and I had visited thirty-seven years ago was gone, and in its place was a modern stone structure with all the facilities and comforts a tourist could ask for.

While I waited for the snack bar to open so I could have breakfast, I called my wife from one of the pay phones. I wanted her to savor this memorable moment with me on the summit of Mount Washington. We had a nostalgic fifteen minutes reliving our honeymoon and the euphoric feelings of thirty-seven years ago. Then after Babs gave me the latest news, we said our good-byes and hung up, and I walked away basking in warm feelings of satisfaction.

Near the snack bar was a rack of t-shirts for sale. One of them read: "I survived the world's worst weather," referring to the icy winds on Mount Washington, which are the strongest ever recorded on earth. I certainly felt like a survivor, having hiked 1,832 miles.

Chapter 23

Hiking the AT's Longest Mile

The steps of a good man are ordered of the Lord.
—Psalm 37:23

Mount Washington to Gorham, New Hampshire

After a hearty breakfast, I purchased two egg salad sandwiches and stowed them in my backpack to eat later. I walked out of the summit building and into the fog, which was still thick. It took some searching, but I found the trail and started hiking north, at one point crossing the tracks that carried the famous, century-old Mount Washington Cog Railway train up and down the mountain. Babs and I had taken that train on our honeymoon, and as it chugged up the mountain, we wondered if we'd ever reach the top. This place was absolutely alive with memories.

The harsh weather followed me as I hiked over the rooftop of Mount Washington. The wind was fierce and wet, the landscape hostile. Whenever I was foolish enough to remove my rain gear, thinking there was a respite, the wild weather would return with such vengeance that I would be wet before I could get my gear back on.

And then I would berate myself for taking it off in the first place. However, in spite of the wild weather, it was exciting to hike this famous mountain.

On August 22, I hiked over Mount Madison, which proved to be a greater challenge than I had expected. Although the weather had improved, the trail was so rocky that it took me six hours to hike a meager three miles. But it was not all in vain because when I stopped for a rest break amid a jumble of rocks with my pack as a cushion for my back, a man in his fifties hiking south appeared on the trail. Thinking he might be from Quebec, I greeted him in French. At that he smiled, took off his pack, sat down, and then began conversing in French.

He said his name was Hugh, and he was a math professor from Quebec. We had a lively discussion about religion, and I was able to share my faith in Christ with this fine gentleman. At the end of our conversation we separated, Hugh hiking south and I heading north. We wished each other happy hiking. We would never see each other again, but that brief time had enriched both our lives and perhaps made an eternal difference.

Almost every day provided opportunities to give hikers the good news of the gospel, and some days there were so many openings that I felt like a one-man evangelism team.

On top of Middle Carter Mountain I stopped for a break. As I snacked on a Snickers bar, a hiker in his twenties approached me and introduced himself as Grasshopper. He was about five feet tall, so his trail name seemed appropriate. Grasshopper was stocky with sturdy legs protruding from his hiking shorts. I was not surprised when he told me he was a construction worker from New York City; I had already guessed his hometown from his Brooklyn accent.

When I offered him a tract, he thanked me and said, "I've been dying for something to read." He explained that he had long ago fled his Catholic upbringing, but the grandeur of the mountains had caused him to consider the existence of God in a way that he never had done before. He even had started praying. Grasshopper was ripe for a witness. The splendor of God's creation all around us was a perfect backdrop as

I talked to this young man about God's love and the salvation revealed in Jesus Christ.

That evening I reached Imp Campsite. I was getting excited. In a few days I would cross into Maine. But before that, I needed to stop in Gorham, New Hampshire, because it had been a long time since my last shower and full meal.

At Imp Campsite I talked with the caretaker, Cody. His passion for the trail was as great as mine, and we talked about many things concerning the AT. We both had read Earl Shaeffer's book *Walking with Spring*, and we discussed that for a while. We talked too about the trials of hiking, such as the fatigue and aching muscles. Our conversation must have inspired him, because as I left Cody, I heard him singing in his tent the hiker's prayer: "If you'll pick 'em up, Lord, I'll put 'em down."

The next day, August 24, 2001, I hiked the eight miles to Gorham, New Hampshire. It was hot as I made my way along Rattle River. I came to a beautiful pond, so inviting that I wanted to strip off my clothes and take a plunge, but it was late in the day, and I had to press on. I promised myself that next time I would yield to the temptation to take a swim.

That day I met an overweight man on the trail, which was unusual because AT hikers are nearly always slim and trim. The thirtyish man was hiking from Maine to Virginia and said that his weight had dropped from 320 pounds to 260. I congratulated him on his achievement and encouraged him to keep up the good work. Although I've never had much of a weight problem, I sympathize with those who do. And I'm sure that if hiking ever becomes a national craze in America, it will go a long way towards reducing the obesity epidemic.

Gorham, New Hampshire, was larger than I'd expected. It easily met all the needs of a hiker and had a large hostel named Hiker's Paradise, a name that promised a bit more than it delivered. There were several rooms for hikers, and I chose a smaller one on the second floor with four bunks but no other occupants for the moment.

Although my original plan was to spend only a night or two in Gorham, I ended up staying a full five days. At the hostel was a large teddy-bear of a man named Bruce, who shuttled hikers to and from the trail, allowing them to slack-pack large sections of the AT. It was an opportunity that I couldn't pass up. After three weeks of hiking, I was weary and welcomed the chance to hike minus my full backpack. Also, I knew that soon I would hit Mahoosuc Notch, the hardest and longest mile on the Appalachian Trail, and if I had to carry a heavy pack over that section, I'd never make it.

My five days in Gorham passed by in a blur. The days started at 4:30 A.M., when I dressed quickly, read a Bible passage, and wolfed down a bowl of oatmeal in the hostel kitchen. Then I staggered out in the dark to meet Bruce and the six or seven other hikers at 5:45 for the trip to the trail. The lucky hikers got to ride in the cab of Bruce's pickup, while the rest rode in the open truck bed and dealt with the cold morning air and the bumpy road. We were a long way from paradise on those trips, but it was part of the adventure, and the hikers—even the older ones like me—took the discomfort in stride.

In the evening, Bruce picked us up at 6:00 at the end of our hike and returned us to the hostel in Gorham. It took a lot of organization and driving on Bruce's part, but he seemed to enjoy it. He had been a long-distance hiker in his younger days, but now, because physical disabilities kept him off the trail, he found satisfaction in helping hikers fulfill their dreams of reaching Katahdin. For that service to others, Bruce had my utmost admiration.

Once we returned to Gorham at the end of the day, it was time to chow down at a restaurant and recover all those calories we had burned on the trail. I developed a daily ritual for this time of day. The hostel had several beaten-up bikes that hikers could use to get around town. I would grab a bike and head to one of the many eating places. However, the road into town was downhill, and all these old bikes had faulty brakes. So I would pray and coast down to a spot where the road turned uphill again and I could brake with my hiking boots on the ground. It was a little scary, but I did it without incident.

While at Paradise, I met a hiker from Florida named Preacher, a Southern Baptist preacher thru-hiking the AT. I immediately felt a bond with this brother in his forties who had a vision similar to mine of reaching AT hikers with the gospel. His approach differed from mine in that he wanted to challenge churches to establish Christian centers along the AT to help hikers and minister to them through love and the truth. Preacher and I had a great time comparing notes and encouraging each other in the work to which God had called us.

On August 27, 2001, my second day of slack-packing, I reached Maine! In the middle of the wilderness, a hand-painted sign appeared before me: "Welcome to Maine. The Way Life Should Be." I couldn't have agreed more. Reaching Maine was another wonderful milestone in God's plan for my life; and this was what He meant my life to be at that point.

I was so happy finally to be in Maine that I felt like dancing, and to celebrate the occasion, I broke open an egg salad sandwich. This was a moment to savor. The sign read: "Springer Mountain—1,877 miles." That's how far I had come. Below it were the words: "Mount Katahdin—281.4 miles." That's the distance that lay between me and "The Great Mountain." I had no illusions about what lay ahead, though, because those remaining miles would be packed with challenges.

THE DREADED NOTCH

My first challenge came two days after crossing the Maine border, when I reached the dreaded Mahoosuc Notch. Ever since the day I had stepped foot on the AT in Georgia in 1992, I'd been apprehensive about Mahoosuc. I had read all the stories of boulders the size of houses and the tremendous difficulty and dangers in hiking "The Appalachian Trail's longest mile."

Mahoosuc Notch lived up to its billing—and then some. It took me three hours to negotiate that one mile. A gracious help the Lord provided was the assistance and encouragement of five younger hikers. Recognizing that a sixty-seven-year-old hiker might run into some problems with Mahoosuc, they invited me to hike that tough mile with them.

Hiking just ahead of me, my five friends warned me of the dangerous places and how best to negotiate them. They also provided encouragement and a lot of good fun and fellowship that helped us all over the exceedingly-difficult places. Even with their help, I fell twice, leaving me with a bruised arm and a skinned left leg. But the injuries were not serious, and we all let out a whoop of delight when we reached the end of Mahoosuc Notch. That awesome notch was one place on the AT to which I had no intention of ever returning, a once-in-a-lifetime experience that I was very thankful to have behind me.

Chapter 24

The Shock of 9/11

You will keep him in perfect peace, whose mind is stayed on you.

—Isaiah 16:3

Gorham, New Hampshire to East Carry Pond

I called Babs several times while I was in Gorham. She planned to drive from Ohio to meet me at the base of Mount Katahdin on September 29, 2001, and Chad would be coming with her. I was excited by that news, which made me all the more eager to reach the finish line and the end of my long journey.

But before that happened, I would have the pleasure of hiking through Maine. I wanted to enjoy this experience for which I had worked so hard—and enjoy it I did. The mountains were as challenging as any I had encountered so far. Although hiking up Old Speck Mountain was a brutal climb of almost 2,000 feet, the rough going was easily matched by the beauty I beheld, and I was rewarded abundantly for my efforts. Not only the mountains, but also the many exquisite ponds in Maine, added so much to my experience on this last leg of my hike.

Millions of Americans dream of hiking the Appalachian Trail, but there I was, actually seeing the dream come true. Why this privilege had been granted me, I didn't know. But I believed with all my heart that this "stroll of a lifetime" was God's idea, and that since my boyhood, He had been preparing me for the experience. I was deeply thankful that I had not missed this incredible adventure because of my unbelief.

Another reason for thanksgiving was that I was in relatively good physical shape. Many of the hikers I'd met wore elastic bandages on legs, knees, and other parts of their bodies, and they popped a lot of ibuprofen pills for pain. These "walking wounded" of the AT were mostly thru-hikers, but as a section hiker, I didn't have those stress injuries. I had scratches and bruises from falls, but my legs, knees, and feet were in good condition. That too was God's grace.

I had heard good things about Saddleback Mountain and was looking forward to climbing it. I was not disappointed. Saddleback was well graded and, to my surprise, relatively easy to climb. Numerous plateaus of rock ledges and balds allow hikers to gaze for long distances and thus have magnificent views of the landscape. I found Saddleback to be very appealing and understood why it is special to many AT hikers. In addition, the perfect weather that day only enhanced my enjoyable and memorable experience.

While climbing Lone Mountain, I followed a mountain stream called Sluice Brook. The weather was stiflingly hot, and I remembered the promise I had made to myself to take a swim if the opportunity presented itself again. When I came upon an enticing and delightful pool of water made by the brook, I took the plunge.

I had met only one or two people on the trail that day, so I felt that I could swim in any condition I chose. So after stripping off my clothes in record time, I jumped into the water. My swim time set a record as well. I lasted six seconds in the ice-cold water—Mississippi one, Mississippi two—before the numbing cold drove me out of the water.

The whole thing, including dressing, was over in a few minutes, but I felt wonderfully refreshed and ready to continue my hike up the mountain. It had been fun too—my first time to skinny-dip since the summers of my boyhood in Warren, Ohio, swimming in the Mahoning River.

That evening, I ended my day far from any campsite or shelter. For want of anything better, I set up my tent in a scrubby woods about twenty feet from the AT. I slept fairly well, but just before dawn, I was awakened by the sound of thundering hoof beats. (Was the Lone Ranger in the area?) As the hoof beats grew louder, I was immediately alert and had visions of being trampled to death in my tent. I grabbed my flashlight, but by the time I rolled out of my tent, the herd—of whatever animals they were—had pounded past me.

Awake now, I stood there pondering what had happened and realized that the hoof beats could only have been moose galloping down the AT. I had been hoping for a moose-sighting. That hadn't happened. Now I consoled myself. I hadn't actually seen moose, but at least I had heard them. My nose-to-nose encounter with a moose would come later.

That evening, at Poplar Ridge shelter, I talked with a hiker named simply LT, who told me of an incident on the trail that disturbed me. A hiker had come to the shelter where LT was staying and decided to make a fire. With no other fuel to start the fire, he proceeded to rip pages out of the shelter Bible! LT said that he and the other hikers stood there astonished by that blatant act of desecration; then quickly, someone gave the man a fire starter. Hearing that story, I couldn't help reflecting that while I and other Christians on the AT were seeking to exalt the Word of God, one man was burning it. Such is the battle that rages between light and darkness—even on the Appalachian Trail.

BELOVED BIGELOW

After admiring the lovely Stratton Pond, I hiked another two miles to the edge of the Bigelow Range. My Maine handbook described the entire range as "the finest between Mount Washington and Katahdin." By the time I had reached the other end of the Bigelow Range, I was in complete agreement.

Maybe it was the strange, stormy weather or the unsurpassed beauty of Bigelow or the sentimental mood I was in, knowing that I was only 180 miles from the end of my journey. It probably was all three, and more, but I felt God's presence in a way I never could describe fully. I would liken Bigelow to Moses' Mount Sinai experience when he talked with God in the clouds and drew nearer to Him than he ever dreamed possible.

After a dark, stormy afternoon, rays of sun penetrated the gray clouds at 5:00 P.M. They broke through in a way that made the rays appear like God's hands reaching down to me. I know I sound like a hopeless mystic here, but the encounter with God was so real, so tremendous, that I gladly would have hiked two thousand miles just for that one mountaintop experience with my Creator and my God. There on Mount Bigelow, my God and I walked together; it was just God and me on that mountain.

My journal entry on September 11, 2001, read:

> Glorious! Rays of sun pierced through dark clouds, giving a beautiful sunset. I felt that magnificent burst of beauty was given to me by the Lord. I had a front row seat to His splendor. Once again, I was an eyewitness of His majesty. It was a foretaste of heaven.

That glorious, otherworldly experience on Bigelow was followed by news so tragic and alarming that it threatened to destroy my peace and plunge me into spiritual darkness. Yet, in the end, even that dark valley experience opened my heart and mind to a new understanding of God's power and purposes in this world.

The morning of September 12, 2001, I hiked past lovely Flagstaff Lake and then proceeded to West Carry Pond, where I stopped to enjoy a leisurely lunch and admire the pristine beauty of Maine. *Indeed,* I said to myself, *this is the way life ought to be.*

That afternoon, I was hiking the remaining five miles to East Carry Pond and was about to step onto a narrow plank walkway that crossed a swamp when I noticed a large man on the other end of the walkway. I knew the plank would not be wide enough for both of us, so I waited at my end until he crossed over.

As the man, in his late thirties, approached me, it appeared that he had been crying. Concerned, I asked, "Is everything all right?"

"Haven't you heard?" the man replied. Then he proceeded to tell me of the terrorist attack the day before, September 11. He said the World Trade Center had been destroyed, as well as part of the Pentagon, with maybe 50,000 people dead.

I was shocked, and for a moment, I wondered if the man was demented. But as he continued talking, I realized that what he told me actually had happened, even though I later learned that some of the details were wrong. The man was so disturbed and so fearful for his family that he'd decided to end his hike and return to his home in New York.

When the hiker had finished his description of the terrorist attack, I felt led to ask him about his relationship with God. It seemed to me to be an appropriate question, given the circumstances. But to my utter amazement, the man became angry. His face reddened, and he turned and stomped off, saying, "I've put my faith in mankind."

I could hardly believe my ears! After the madness that "mankind" just had committed in New York City, this man was placing his bets on humanity. I was flabbergasted but managed to shout to the man as he walked down the trail, "Look to God; don't look to man."

Less than an hour later, still greatly troubled by the news of the terrorist attack, I came to East Carry Pond. The sun was setting, and I decided to camp on a narrow stretch of beach that bordered the pond. The mild weather held not a hint of rain, so I stretched out my ground cloth and then my sleeping bag.

Down the shoreline, about the length of a football field, I saw another person. I walked toward him and discovered it was Mr. Pink, a red-haired young man I had met at a shelter the night before. Mr. Pink was the picture of despair, and when I asked him how things were going, he replied, "All I can think about is the terrorist attack."

He seemed open to talk, so I sat beside him on the sand and shared some thoughts from Psalm 46, emphasizing the words, "Be still and know that I am God."

In contrast to the humanist I had encountered in the swamp, Mr. Pink was receptive to the message of faith in God. He thanked me for the words from the Bible that I had shared with him. When I got up to leave, he already was reading the gospel tract I had given him.

I returned to my campsite on the beach, and after a light supper, I bedded down for the night. It was already dark, and I lay on my back a long while looking up at the night sky. What I saw was beautiful beyond description. Above me, brilliant stars sparkled like diamonds.

Several of them shot across the sky like rockets on the Fourth of July. A sliver of moon cast its light over the lake, and highlighted powder blue and white puffy clouds drifting across the heavens. Several feet from me, small waves from the lake gently lapped the shore. God's world had never seemed so peaceful.

As I lay on the beach, I was overwhelmed by the stark contrast between my idyllic surroundings and the awful destruction in New York City. In the Maine wilderness I felt worlds away from chaos and hate-filled terrorists. Yet, I reminded myself, at that very moment, America was under attack, and thousands were weeping over lost loved ones. I couldn't change that tragic situation, but I could pray.

There on my little beach, I spent several hours interceding in prayer for our president and for all in authority, for grieving families and for those still trapped under steel and stone. I prayed for a mighty moving of God in America.

When I looked at my watch, it was almost midnight. Committing my family to the Lord, I drifted off to sleep with a renewed confidence that the One who had created a world so beautiful was watching over it and bringing to pass His divine plans and purposes.

Chapter 25

An Evening with
Mr. Backpacker

The fear of the Lord is the beginning of knowledge.
—Proverbs 1:7

East Carry Pond to Horseshoe Canyon Shelter

CROSSING THE KENNEBEC

For hikers, Kennebec River has a scary reputation. More than one hiker has lost his or her life trying to cross against its powerful current. It is a wide river, and its depth can be deceptive when a dam upriver is released. Kennebec was the next challenge on my quest for Katahdin, and fortunately, there was now a canoe-shuttle to take hikers across the river.

As I walked down the last hill to the Kennebec River, I was startled by a voice. Seated on the ground with his back against a tree was Steve Longely. Steve was in his forties, broad-shouldered, and had the tanned look of an outdoorsman. This was all reassuring, as he was the man responsible for canoeing me across a swift and highly-unpredictable river. I shook Steve's hand, introduced myself, and thanked him for being there.

Steve, the owner of a hiker hostel in Caratunk, was also the son of a former governor of Maine. He was friendly and seemed to enjoy his work of helping hikers. Steve loaded my backpack into the canoe, and after he explained the details of our crossing, we launched out on an exciting ride across the swift Kennebec River. I was thankful I didn't have to ford the river on my own. Steve gave me a paddle too, but I'm not sure how much I contributed to the effort. Above the noise of the water, we talked about the terrorist attack. His cousin had lost his life in one of the twin towers, and in a few days, Steve would attend his memorial service.

When we reached the other side of the river, Steve took me in his truck to the hiker hostel in Caratunk, Maine. The first thing I did was find a telephone and call my wife. While my call was going through, I couldn't help wondering if this would be the end of my hike for 2001. Would Babs be so upset that she would need me to return to Ohio? Although her needs were my first priority, I also deeply wanted to finish my hike. I was only 151 miles from the great goal, and I was not sure that I ever would return to the AT if I didn't reach Katahdin that year. Circumstances as well as age were breathing down my neck.

I needn't have worried. My wife's voice was calm, and she had the Lord's peace about the terrorist attack. My leaving the trail was never even mentioned. Her main concern was helping her elderly parents get back to Ohio from Newfoundland, where they'd been stranded while returning from Europe on the day of the attack. Once again, my wife had shown her strength and come through a trying time with flying colors.

The next morning, Steve shuttled me back to the trail. As I retrieved my backpack from his truck and said "good-bye," I assured him that he would be in my prayers as he attended the memorial service for his cousin. I then turned northward and to my pursuit of the Holy Grail called Katahdin.

From Caratunk, it was uphill—not terribly steep but still tiring. When I reached the foot of Mount Pleasant, I decided to call it a day, even though I had hiked only six miles. I would attack the intimidating mountain the following day when I was fresh.

An Evening with Mr. Backpacker

I headed for Mount Pleasant Lean-to, which was just off the trail. The tall, male hiker who had arrived just ahead of me introduced himself as Artic Fox from Michigan. Artic Fox explained that he had once swum in a Michigan lake in October, and from that frigid experience he had acquired his trail name. He had started his hike in Georgia the previous April, and now in mid-September, he was close to completing his thru-hike. As we were both nearing the end of our hikes, we felt a natural kinship.

We set up camp and cooked our suppers over small gas stoves. We talked as we ate. From my trail experiences I had learned that it doesn't take hikers long to get acquainted. Between mouthfuls of backpacker stew, he told me a few things about his life. He was in his forties, a college grad, divorced, and the father of two sons.

Before long we began talking about God. By the warmth of an after-supper campfire, we spent almost two hours discussing what it means to be a Christian. At one time he had been in a Bible study group but had long since abandoned it, and now, he confided, sinful habits controlled his life. He listened thoughtfully as I explained truths from the Bible and their importance in our lives.

Finally, shivering from a cold front that had moved in, we said "good-night." Before retreating to his tent, Artic Fox thanked me for the evening and said, "There are going to be changes in my life."

I crawled into my sleeping bag, and as I watched the dying embers of our campfire, I felt a deep peace. My evening with Artic Fox bore all the marks of a divinely-arranged encounter.

On September 16, I hiked thirteen miles. I was happy with the longer mileage. Because of rough terrain during the last few weeks, many days had been limited to only seven or eight miles of hiking, so it felt good to once again cover a respectable distance.

Horseshoe Canyon

At Horseshoe Canyon Shelter that evening, I met an older hiker who, in my opinion, deserved his trail name, Mr. Backpacker. Because of my own imperfections in backpacking, I admire hikers who are well-organized and have honed their backpacking skills to near perfection.

Mr. Backpacker had thru-hiked the AT at age seventy-two, after having already section hiked the entire trail three times. He had climbed all of the peaks over 5,000 feet in New York and North Carolina and estimated that in all, he had hiked 50,000 miles. At age seventy-eight, his erect, six-foot-two-inch frame was still capable of doing fifteen-mile days. He carried a minimum of weight and had designed and constructed much of his hiking gear. He seemed completely at ease in the wilderness. As far as long-distance hiking was concerned, Mr. Backpacker had it all together.

As we sat eating our suppers together that evening, he with his back against one shelter wall and I leaning against the opposite one, Mr. Backpacker recounted one of his backpacking adventures, an experience that I could tell still haunted him.

He was in New York, hiking with his best friend, with whom he had hiked for twenty years. They were camped for the night when a violent storm hit, producing five tornadoes that passed over them. Torrential rain from the storm had swollen the stream next to their campsite into a raging river, and crossing it was the only way to safety. Fearing for their lives, they plunged into the stream but were soon swept off their feet and carried downstream.

Certain that he was being carried to his death, Mr. Backpacker grabbed the roots of a tree and managed to hang on, and eventually, he climbed out of the water. But his friend was nowhere in sight, so Mr. Backpacker ran to the nearest road and stopped a motorist, who contacted the police. He and the motorist returned to look for his friend. And after searching for a long time, Mr. Backpacker found him face down in the water, his pack still on his back. He had drowned.

As he finished the story, I could tell that the passing years had not erased the sorrow of losing his best friend. After a moment of silence, I took the liberty of asking my elderly friend if it had been he who had lost his life in that terrible flood, would he have gone to heaven. He replied that although he considered himself a Christian, he believed that only parts of the Bible were inspired. My impression was that he was a skeptic in spiritual matters.

I quoted Scripture to Mr. Backpacker and outlined God's plan of salvation, explaining that we need to acknowledge our sins, turn from them, and put our faith in Christ, who was crucified for us. He listened politely, but I could detect no positive response to the gospel on his part. Shortly after, our evening ended.

The next morning as I was leaving the shelter, I gave Mr. Backpacker a tract. He seemed moved and thanked me. Taking my hand, he said with some emotion, "May our paths cross again." As I shouldered my pack and headed down the trail, that was my prayer—that Mr. Backpacker and I would indeed meet again . . . in heaven.

Chapter 26

The One-Hundred-Mile Wilderness

I will even make a road in the wilderness.

—Isaiah 48:19

Horseshoe Canyon Shelter to
Carl Newhall Shelter

Monson, Maine, was my next destination, and then I would enter what hikers call "The One Hundred Mile Wilderness." I wondered how much wilder the wilderness could get, and I would soon find out.

Maybe because it was on the edge of a large wilderness, or perhaps because there were hiker tents here and there and people seemed to be coming and going, Monson felt like a frontier town. All that was missing were cowboys, a saloon with dancing girls, and horse-drawn wagons riding down the main street.

I headed for Shaw's boarding house, the most popular hiker hostel in Monson. Keith and Pat Shaw greeted me warmly, and in no time, I was settled into one of the private rooms. I enjoyed the friendly ambiance at Shaw's and ate with gusto the large servings of delicious food that they served. They seemed to know that northbound hikers needed to store up calories for the lean days ahead.

I watched the evening news on the small TV in my room. President Bush gave a press conference with the caption "America Under Attack." It was evident that Americans were badly shaken, and I prayed that many might turn to God in that time of crisis. In my devotions I read, "God rules all the nations, God sits on his holy throne" (Ps. 67:8). The world was coming apart, but God wasn't.

I was up early the next morning, repacking a fresh supply of food for the hundred-mile wilderness. After a large breakfast, I said "good-bye" to the Shaws and headed for the trail. The hiking was glorious over mountains and along mountain streams. In my journal I wrote:

> I look over miles of trees turning fantastic colors. The sun is
> warm, and I am the happiest man in the world.

I felt on top of the world—until I came to the ford at Big Wilson Stream. There the trail seemed to disappear. I could find no more white blazes for the continuation of the trail. Then I saw the next one—on the other side of the roaring Big Wilson Stream! The first words that came out of my mouth were, "They've got to be kidding!" I couldn't believe that the trail makers expected me to ford that swift, surging current. It looked at least two feet deep in the middle and as wide as a football field. I felt led into a dangerous trap—betrayed.

I looked around for another option but saw none. If I wanted to hike the Appalachian Trail, I would have to cross Big Wilson. Seldom on my hike had I felt so vulnerable; all my confidence had been swept away by that wild stream.

I prayed, asking the Lord for His protection and help in getting across Big Wilson. Then I plunged in. I noticed immediately how slippery the rocks were. I tried stepping up on boulders that were higher, but I quickly realized doing so was too dangerous. My only hope was to keep my feet planted on the streambed, even if that meant exposing myself to the full force of the current.

I was very thankful that I had hiking poles because they gave me at least a measure of stability. But even with my poles, in the middle of the stream, I came very close several times to losing my balance and being carried downstream by the current. That would have meant, at the very least, that I and everything in my pack would have been soaked. It was not a happy prospect for a long-distance hiker in the wilderness!

With water hitting me full force and mid-thigh, I kept plodding and praying, step after step, until I finally reached the other shore with great relief. I hiked uphill a short distance and came to Big Wilson Shelter, where I got rid of some of the water I had collected. I poured the water out of my boots and wrung what seemed like a bucketful of water from my heavy hiking socks. I knew that the remaining water eventually would be squeezed out as I walked.

Before I left the shelter, I checked the shelter log. There I read the entry of another hiker, who the day before had been overcome by the current and fallen into Big Wilson. Everything he had, including his camera, was soaked. I felt sympathy for the poor fellow and gratitude for my safe crossing.

MEETING THE MOOSE

Every two-thousand-miler has a secret desire to sight a bear and a moose during his hike. Seeing these creatures gives legitimacy to the experience, and then bragging rights will be his portion. He will be able to speak about his hike with authority and walk with the swagger of the anointed. The rest of his life he will be able to describe that experience to awestruck listeners and admirers. Grandchildren and great-grandchildren will sit at his feet while he tells them of the dangerous encounters. This is why the hiker who never meets a bear or a moose feels somehow cheated.

By this time, I was feeling among the cheated. I had hiked 2,000 miles without one clear bear sighting (although, no doubt, many bears had seen me). I lamented this fact and hoped that now that I was in Maine my reputation could be salvaged by an honest-to-goodness moose sighting. The way it happened was beyond anything I could have imagined.

On the morning of September 22, at 6:15, I was sitting in Carl Newhall Shelter eating a typical meager breakfast, Cheerios® and dry toast with jam. Alone in the silent forest, I suddenly heard a loud thump on the side of the shelter. *Strange,* I thought, *that another hiker would be arriving at this early hour of the morning.*

But it wasn't a hiker. Around the corner of the shelter, not more than ten feet from me, appeared a huge bull moose with eight-point antlers. We were almost eyeball-to-eyeball, and I was not comfortable with the closeness. I had read somewhere that more people are killed by moose each year than by bears. If that bull moose had decided to charge, I would have had no way to escape.

The moose and I stared at each other for a full seven seconds. I didn't move a muscle; I was paralyzed! Finally, to my great relief, that magnificent beast retreated a couple of steps and galloped back into the forest. I sat there a few minutes, trying to digest what had just happened. The Lord certainly had answered my prayer for a moose sighting. But the encounter had been much closer than I had anticipated, or desired. Then I had an encouraging thought: *Wow, what a moose story I'll have to tell my grandkids!*

I was now only 78.6 miles from Katahdin. I detected a subtle change, a sadness, in the hikers I was meeting. In the shelter logs I read both excited entries and words of regret. For the thru-hikers, even more than for the sections hikers, it was the end of a long adventure. For six months they had been walking "The Dream," and now that dream was coming to an end. The whole goal of their existence during the past six months had been to "climb Katahdin." They soon would reach that goal, but it would mean the end of a vision, and the end of friendships made during their hike. Just reading the logs gave me twinges of sadness.

To overcome the melancholy, I sang. One song in particular that lifted my spirits was "We're on the Homeward Trail." That little chorus reminded me that my ultimate goal was not Katahdin but heaven. Reaching my long-awaited AT goal was only a faint reflection of the joyful meeting with Christ I would have at the end of my life. That thought put a new spring into my step.

On September 24, I had an accident that almost put an end to my journey. It was the worst fall of my hike. In good spirits that day, I foolishly jumped up on a large rock that I encountered on the path. The rock was wet, as were my boots, and my foot slipped off the rock.

I landed on my left side, injuring my hip and arm. I was able to get up off the ground, but my bloodied left arm hurt, and I had pain in my hip. For the next two days, I walked with a limp. I was grateful that I hadn't hit my head or smashed a knee, as serious damage to either would have put me out of action. Praise God, I was still moving toward Katahdin!

Chapter 27

The Euphoria of the Final Miles

And his heart took delight in the ways of the Lord.
—2 Chronicles 17:6

Carl Newhall Shelter to White House Wilderness Camp

As I began the last fifty miles of my journey, the glory of fall was all around me. It was in part my reward for all of the exhaustion and bruises of 2,000 miles of hiking. And what a reward! The vibrant colors and feelings of nostalgia resonated with my personality. Here I was in the wilderness of Maine, one of the most wonderful places in the world to view the mysteries of autumn. At times I walked in a dream, not comprehending that I was actually in Maine during autumn. I laughed, cried, shouted praises to the Lord, and sang songs of love to my Creator-God. I was in heaven.

Yet earth still had its claims on me: I was running low on food, and I felt a need to touch base with civilization. According to my guidebook, in that hundred-mile wilderness was a place called the White House Wilderness Camp. I decided it would be my next destination. There I could take a shower, resupply with food, and gather my strength for the final push to Katahdin.

193

The trail to the camp was historical as well as beautiful. It was part of the original Appalachian Trail. I was inspired as I meditated on that slice of history and those hikers of the late 1930s who had followed this very trail—what were they like; what were their hopes, dreams, and fears. Were they worried about Hitler and the outbreak of a second world war? Those hikers were gone now. Their day had passed. What had been their relationships with God? I fervently hoped that they had worshiped Him as they trod this trail.

After hiking 1.2 miles, I came to large Pemadumcook Lake and a boat landing. I saw the camp in the distance. I discovered an air-horn that would let White House Camp know that a hiker needed to be ferried across the lake to the camp.

I pushed the button on the horn firmly (only one blast, please) and almost leaped into the lake! The noise was deafening, and echoing off the water, it must have been heard for miles. It worked, and within three minutes, a motorboat was speeding toward me.

The driver introduced himself as Bill Ware. In his late forties, good-looking, stocky, and with graying hair, Bill seemed almost shy. *Typical Maine personality,* I thought, *friendly but taciturn.* The little conversation we had ended when the boat roared off across the lake toward the camp.

The first thing I noticed as I climbed out of the boat was an American flag being whipped by the wind on a nearby pole. As I hoisted my backpack, Bill directed me up the hill toward one of several large buildings. For a wilderness camp, the setting was attractive, even civilized.

As I walked onto the porch of the main building, two large, friendly dogs greeted me, and a sign informed hikers to remove their boots. Once inside, I was greeted by Linda, Bill's wife, who welcomed me with a warm smile. On the walls were trophies of a deer, a bear, and all the usual décor that makes up a hunting lodge. That ambiance, coupled with the huge cheeseburger I ordered, made me feel right at home.

After my meal, which was so welcome after the starvation diet I had endured over the last two days, Bill took me to a rustic cabin on the lakeshore. The cabin had four small bedrooms, a small kitchen, and a lounge with the usual well-worn couch and easy chairs. A wide window looked out on the lake. I was delighted. There was even a shortwave radio that allowed me to keep up with news of the terrorist attack. After I got settled in the cabin, I took my first shower in seven days and hoped all that dirt would not clog the drain.

Outside the cabin and at the foot of the lake, I discovered a primitive washing machine, which was operated by hand—even the wringer—and used cold lake water. After using the washing machine, my clothes were not sparkling clean, but their condition was improved.

Using that old wringer brought back memories of my boyhood and the old washing machine my mother used in our basement with its crumbling walls. The simple routine never varied. While she pressed the clothes through the ringer, I sat watching on the basement stairs, or I would help her. But we always talked. Looking back, I realized that my mother, Mardell, cherished those moments. I guess I did too. During those washing-wringing sessions, my mother passed on important wisdom for my life. Sixty years later, I thanked God for her counsel. The example of her courage and grit during the Great Depression was an encouragement to me on my hike.

There was no telephone service on the island. But Bill and Linda had a cell phone, which they let me use. The only problem was that it cost twenty dollars a minute! I decided to bite the bullet and call my wife to finalize our plans for meeting five days later at the foot of Mount Katahdin. Babs was frustrated with only a minute to talk, but we were able to settle on our meeting place and time. Chad would be with her and would climb the mountain with me. That was comforting news because I had not been looking forward to a solo climb to the summit of Katahdin.

After a big breakfast the following morning, Bill returned me to the boat landing. I had been impressed with the White House Wilderness Camp, a wilderness-lover's dream. Once again, I vowed I would return someday. There were so many fantastic places I wanted to share in the coming years with my wife, my sons, and my grandchildren.

Saturday, September 27, three days from the end of my journey, I tented on Nesuntabunt Mountain. My tent was only a couple of yards from a rock ledge that offered an outstanding view of Katahdin, my coveted goal for the last nine years. As there was no one else on the mountain that evening, I had the beautiful vista all to myself. It was a special moment, and I was grateful for the solitude.

After supper, I crawled out on the rock ledge that looked out not only on Katahdin but also on Hahmakanta Lake far below me. The lake glistened like a jewel set in the foreground of my panoramic painting.

On the lake a mile below me, I saw two tiny sailboats. Everything was still, not even the wind was blowing. Then to my surprise, I heard faint and faraway sounds, and I realized that the sounds were voices drifting up to me from the occupants of the small sailboats. Strangely, I felt a link to those people, whom I couldn't see because of distance but whose voices I could hear. The people on the sailboats were like me; they had lives, dreams, crises. Although I would never meet them, in a sense, I knew them because I had heard their voices. We were connected. Was I not, I reasoned, in some way connected with everyone in the world? As darkness descended on my little mountain perch, I prayed for more of God's love and concern for people all over the world.

Chapter 28

Bridge over Troubled Waters

When you pass through the waters, I will be with you.
—Isaiah 43:2

White House Wilderness Camp to Baxter State Park

I was only two days from the end of the journey now, and with the obvious exception of Mount Katahdin, I thought that all of my challenges were behind me. Dreamer! I still had one more stiff test ahead of me.

The notation in my guidebook said, "Nesowadnehunk Stream may be difficult in high water." "Difficult" was an understatement—"impossible" would have been more accurate. The torrent raging before me took my breath away.

The euphoria I had been feeling the past week vanished. I was only two days from realizing a long-standing dream, and now this. The direction of the white blazes that marked the trail was all too clear; to reach my goal, I had to cross that surging mass of water. Once again I felt betrayed by the AT planners, even though it really wasn't their fault.

The abundant September rains of the past several weeks had turned peaceful New England streams into raging torrents. Wading across Nesowadnehunk was out of the question; I couldn't pronounce it, much less cross it! The force of the current was too powerful for me even to consider that option. I would be swept off my feet and carried downstream the moment I put my foot in the water. I was less than ten miles from Katahdin, but if I wanted to finish my hike, I would have to find a way to cross that stream.

Just then, I noticed a "bridge" to my left. Some trail maintenance workers must have laid a plank that reached across the stream to the opposite bank. I made my way downstream to look it over. The plank-bridge was about fifteen feet long. Under normal circumstances, crossing this bridge would be a mere skip, hop, and a jump. But this was not a normal circumstance, and I would be putting my life on the line in covering that short distance.

I stepped on the end of the plank to measure how wide it was. Exactly the width of my size-ten hiking boots pressed tightly together—only eight inches wide! The expression "no room for error" took on a whole new meaning.

Added to the risk factor was my acrophobia—fear of heights. I had fallen off a garage roof when I was ten, breaking my wrist and knocking myself unconscious. Ever since then, just looking out the window of a four-story building produces butterflies in my stomach and sometimes dizziness.

The drop from the plank bridge to the cataract below was only about ten feet, but it was high enough to activate my acrophobia, especially when I contemplated what my fate would be if I fell off. If I lost my balance while crossing the plank (entirely possible when you're carrying a forty-pound backpack) and tumbled into that raging caldron of water, my chances of survival would be slim. I would be smashed against the rocks and drowned, the weight of my pack pulling me under the water. This already had happened to a disturbing number of hikers at other AT crossings. Swollen, out-of-control streams are a hiker's greatest enemy in Maine. I searched along the bank of the roaring stream, looking for another option, but I found none. There was only one way to get to the other side; I would have to walk the plank.

Reluctantly, I returned to my "bridge over troubled water," the deafening noise of the surging water below me only increasing my apprehension. After tightening the straps on my pack so that the weight wouldn't shift and gripping my hiking poles, I began to inch across the plank. Visions of Blondin, the famous French tightrope walker, balancing his way across Niagara Falls came to mind. Blondin at least had a cheering crowd watching, but no fans were on hand to witness my exploit, or my disaster. (*Why*, I berated myself, *am I always alone at these dangerous moments?*)

I reached the middle of the board. I didn't dare look down. But even without looking down at the watery death below, I felt panic sweeping over me. My hands gripping the hiking poles were clammy, a familiar sinking feeling seized the pit of my stomach, and my legs refused to move, as if glued to the plank. Then my head started spinning. Was I going to black out, here?

In desperation I cried out, like Peter, "Lord, save me!"

The Lord heard my cry. Slowly the panic loosened its grip on me, and I was able to take a small step, and then another, until finally I reached the safety of the opposite bank. I dropped my pack and fell to the ground. I was emotionally drained but very thankful to the Lord.

An insight came to me from that wild stream crossing: God often allows older Christians to endure severe testing in their later years. Older saints imagine that because they are near the end of life's journey, the remaining path will be easy. That's often not true. A loving Father allows them to go through tough trials to demonstrate before a watching world the depth of their faith. In the process, they experience, as Churchill put it, "their finest hour." Those end-of-life trials allow God to showcase His power.

My euphoria returned and was now, in fact, reaching its peak. It was an emotional high hard to describe. All of the sweat, bruised muscles, strained ligaments, hunger, depression, torment from insects, danger from rattlesnakes, and a thousand other hardships were now on the verge of producing a great triumph—the conquest of Katahdin and the completion of the Appalachian Trail. I observed the same feelings in my fellow hikers. The dream of all dreams was in sight, and intoxication was in the air! A young woman ran past me, and after excusing herself, said, "I'm so excited!"

I understood because I, too, was excited. Only a few miles from Katahdin and I felt like laughing and crying at the same time. It was a feeling unlike any other I had ever felt. A lifetime of emotions surged in my breast, and I seemed to fly through the air, my feet barely touching the ground. My heart bubbled over with thanksgiving, and once again, I bellowed out my theme song of the last twenty miles: "We're on the homeward trail . . . singing, singing, everybody singing, going home."

When I reached Baxter State Park on September 29, I checked in at the park office at Daicey Pond Campground. A park ranger questioned me and several other hikers about our journeys: the year we had started our AT hike and details of our completion. Sensing our strong emotions, the ranger was courteous and congratulated us on our achievement. I appreciated very much his attitude. To weary sojourners, feeling elation and sadness at the same time, kindness and a smile go a long way.

Chapter 29

The End of
the Journey

He has done all things well.

—Mark 7:37

Daicy State Park to the Summit of
Mount Katahdin

After leaving the park office, I walked the last two and a half miles to Katahdin Stream Campground, where I was scheduled to meet Babs and Chad at 4:00 P.M. I walked those last miles slowly. As I expected, there was a sweet sadness to the last walk before climbing Katahdin. The experience of a lifetime was coming to an end.

At Katahdin Stream Campground, I was surrounded by other hikers who were emotional about their finish. Some were doing as I was—waiting for family members to join them for the celebration.

At 4:10, I saw a flash of red as our Chrysler Concord came into sight and pulled up in front of me. Babs and Chad jumped out, and the next moments were given over to joyful hugs and kisses. It had been two months since Babs and I had embraced, and I was bubbly with joy that my wife and son were here for the grand finale of my AT hike, the climb up Mount Katahdin.

Babs had reserved rooms for us at Big Moose Inn, so I threw my pack in the trunk, and we drove to the Inn. Big Moose was rustic and comfortable, but my concerns about the climb up Katahdin robbed me of a good night's sleep. Would the good weather continue? Would there be a wait because other hikers arrived ahead of time? Would I be up to the physical challenge?

The clang of our alarm awoke me at 4:00 the next morning. The date was September 30, 2001. Chad and I met in the kitchen of the Inn, along with several other sleepy-eyed hikers who were going to challenge the mighty mountain that day. Rangers had warned us to get to the base of the mountain early because the line might be long and only a certain number of climbers would be allowed on the summit on a given day. We ate a big breakfast, knowing that we would need a lot of energy for the climb.

By the time we finished our breakfast and readied our packs, Babs was awake and dressed. We piled our packs into the car and headed to Katahdin, about ten miles away. The air was frigid, and fog made visibility difficult, but at 5:15 A.M., we arrived at Baxter State Park. The park ranger at the entrance gate shivered as she asked us about our plans to hike Katahdin. With her questions answered, she waved us on.

I was relieved that there were only a dozen cars ahead of us when we arrived at the park. *So far, so good*, I thought. We were getting an early start. I knew that I would not be setting any speed records for climbing Katahdin that day. My only goal was to get to the top, snap the photos, and make the return trip without any injuries.

By 6:30 there was enough light to begin our assent, and the three of us huddled for warmth and prayer. Our photos taken there show us cringing from the cold but beaming with excitement. Before us was the climb of all climbs; the experience I had been looking forward to for nine years finally had arrived.

Chad and I carried daypacks, but Babs had no pack at all because she only was hiking the first mile with us. When we reached Katahdin Stream Falls, we decided it was time to separate while the hiking was still easy. Chad and I would continue climbing, and my wife would return to our car. Having Babs hike with us that first mile to the summit meant more to me than I ever could have expressed in words.

She, more than anyone else, had made The Hike possible. I gave her a final kiss and a hug, hoping that the look in my eyes conveyed the love and appreciation I felt for her. My wife turned and headed back to the trailhead, and Chad and I took determined steps toward the summit of Katahdin.

Climbing that next mile after Katahdin Stream Falls was relatively easy. Then we came to a sheer mass of rocks that seemed to reach to heaven itself, and we felt small and insignificant before this terrible tower of boulders. But we reasoned that if others had climbed them, there must be a way through this seemingly-impossible impasse.

So up we climbed, at some points pulling ourselves up on iron bars that had been fixed in the rocks. Had it not been for Chad's moral support, I'm not sure I would have made it. How gracious was the Lord to provide my son and his help in this last and hardest of all AT climbs. The God who had helped me in a thousand difficulties over 2,000 miles was proving faithful to the very end of my hike.

Once we passed the huge boulders, the climbing was easier. The sun was shining, and we talked animatedly as we hiked past Thoreau Spring. A wooden sign told us that we were only a mile from the summit of Katahdin. One mile left! It had all come to this—all of the hardships, sweat, trials, joys, and adventures had brought me to the last mile.

The hikers around us seemed to be more thoughtful now as we approached the end. Some who had been giddy an hour before were now quiet. More than a few, no doubt, were dreading the end of the greatest adventure of their lives. Perhaps they were agonizing over the return to civilization and their old routines.

And all at once, the famous wooden Katahdin sign came into sight, and the last mile had ended. I looked at my watch: 12:10. We had been hiking five hours and forty minutes. The Katahdin sign, rough and weathered, read:

Katahdin—Northern Terminus of the Appalachian Trail

What simple, sweet, satisfying words. As did most of the two dozen hikers around me, I went up and touched the weathered sign, the tangible evidence of our triumph.

I turned and noticed a new hiker arriving, a bearded young man. He was weeping, overcome with emotion. From the conversation around me, I gathered that the young man had gone through a traumatic experience, perhaps the loss of a friend, and the completion of his thru-hike had a sad, symbolic meaning for him. A hiker from our group walked out to the tearful man and embraced him. It was a touching moment.

Strangely, my own emotions at the end were low-key. Because I'd had so many emotional highs and lows during my 2,000 miles, when I stood on Katahdin at last, I was simply very thankful. Chad and I gave each other a congratulatory hug, took our photos, and sat down on the ground to thank God for His goodness and eat the sandwiches we'd brought.

At 1:00 P.M., after a last, lingering look at the surrounding panorama, we started down the mountain slowly, remembering the hiker's adage: "Climbing up the mountain hikers get tired, climbing down the mountain, they get hurt." We talked little as we worked our way down the mountain; instead, we meditated and concentrated on avoiding injury.

It was nearly 6:00 P.M. by the time we reached Katahdin Stream. The early fall darkness of Maine already was upon us, and we felt the cold creeping into our bones. Both of us were dead tired and limping from the difficult descent. We might have experienced melancholy but for my beloved wife, who was coming up the path to meet us with a wide smile. Her appearance swept away any post-hike letdown. I love her more than I ever could express.

We fell into each other's arms. Then, after giving Babs a brief recap of our exploit, the three of us walked arm in arm back to the car in the sharp cold and gathering darkness. My heart was overflowing.

The adventure of a lifetime was over, but I had the feeling that the blessings from my hike of the Appalachian Trail were just beginning. The future would be as bright as the promises of God.

Epilogue

At times my eyes fall on the long map taped to the wall of my study—a map of the entire Appalachian Trail—and I ask myself, "Is it possible I really hiked the whole thing?" I know the answer, of course, but eight years after the fact, I marvel that I walked 2,160 miles through the wilderness—from Georgia to Maine—a trek of five million steps. It still seems like a feat completely beyond me. And it was. God's power alone enabled me to do it.

And that, I believe, is the message of my AT story: God calls ordinary Christians to accomplish great things—things completely beyond their human capacities. Our God always calls us to impossible missions. And it is only as we venture beyond our limits in answering His call that we can do the great things God has planned for us in this life. It was this conviction that led Paul to write, "I can do all things through Christ who strengthens me" (Phil. 4:13).

The Appalachian Trail changed my life. I am more willing to take risks in God's service than before. My faith is stronger, and my vision for youth evangelism is greater. Seven years ago (I was sixty-nine; somehow age seems less a factor to me since my hike), Babs and I started a youth Bible club through our church with Word of Life International. Sunday mornings I teach a class that includes many teenage boys from a nearby drug rehab program. It has been exciting to see young people come to Christ through these ministries. We return to France nearly every year for a ministry of preaching and encouraging believers. Last year, beginning in the north, I started a prayer-walk across France. The opportunities to witness were many, and I may continue my walk all the way to Bordeaux in the south of France, a distance of 400 miles. Stay tuned.

I still hike whenever I can get away with Babs or with our sons. Chad, with his wife Tricia, is a real estate investor. He has made three mission trips to India and three to other countries. Mark, a partner in Florida's third largest law firm, finds time to compete in triathlons and Iron-Man races. He has made mission trips to Guatemala and is active in youth work. David, in a very demanding job as a computer software consultant for major companies, releases tension by kayaking swift rivers and sky-diving.

I'm praying our six grandchildren will read the story of their Grandpa Anderson's Appalachian Trail hike and be challenged to venture beyond their own limits in attempting great things for God. Onward!

Books about the Appalachian Trail

Brill, David. *As Far As The Eye Can See—Reflections of an Appalachian Trail Hike*. Nashville: Rutledge Hill Press, 1990.

Cornelius, Madelaine. *Katahdin With Love*. Lookout Mt, TN: Milton Publishing Company, 1991.

Curren, Jan D. *The Appalachian Trail: Journey of Discovery*. H. Highland City, FL: Rainbow Books, Inc., 1991.

Deeds, Jean. *There are Mountains to Climb*. Indianapolis: Silverwood Press, 1996.

Garvey, Edward B. *Appalachian Hiker II*. Oakton, VA: Appalachian Books, 1971.

Garvey, Edward B. *The New Appalachian Trail*. Birmingham: Menasha Ridge Press, 1987.

Irwin, Bill. *Blind Courage*. Waco, TX: WRS Publishing, 1992.

Logue, Victoria and Frank. *The Appalachian Trail Backpacker's Planning Guide*. Birmingham: Menasha Ridge Press, 1991.

Shaffer, Earl V. *Walking With Spring*. Harpers Ferry, WV: Appalachian Trail Conference, 1983.

All these books can be purchased from:

Appalachian Trail Conservancy
P.O. Box 807
Harpers Ferry,
West Virginia 25425

Call (304) 535-6331

Website: www.appalachiantrail.org.

WinePressPublishing
Great Books, Defined.

To order additional copies of this book call:
1-877-421-READ (7323)
or please visit our website at
www.WinePressbooks.com

If you enjoyed this quality custom-published book,
drop by our website for more books and information.

www.winepresspublishing.com
"Your partner in custom publishing."